ALAN DHILLON & RICHARD DHILLON

Merch That Works

Amplify Your Brand, Engage Customers, and Boost Sales with Strategic Merchandise

First edition

Contents

IMPORTANT – READ THIS FIRST

Hi, we're Alan Dhillon & Richard Dhillon from Probos Promotions, and we're grateful you took the opportunity to get this book.

We've been in the promotional branded merchandise industry for over 20 years. In that time, we've seen every mistake, every misconception, and every lost opportunity when it comes to using branded merchandise effectively. Time and time again, business owners, marketers, and sales professionals struggle to make their promotional products work for them. That's why we put together this much-publicised book—to clear the confusion and show you the power of strategic merchandise done right.

After all, maybe you've spent thousands on promotional items, only to watch them get tossed away, ignored, or forgotten. You had high hopes—thinking your brand would be in front of your customers every day—but instead, your efforts fell flat. No engagement. No impact. Just wasted money.

Maybe you've been overwhelmed by the sheer number of options available—pens, mugs, tote bags, tech gadgets. The choices seem endless, and every supplier promises "the best results." But how do you know what really works? How do you ensure your merchandise doesn't just blend into the noise?

Or maybe you've even tried to launch a campaign, only to find that your promotional items didn't align with your brand, didn't excite your audience, and ultimately failed to generate any real return on investment. Instead of creating a memorable brand experience, your merchandise became just another forgettable freebie.

And look, I get it, it's not fair.

The truth is, you're not alone. It seems most are becoming a victim of poorly planned, ineffective promotional merchandise campaigns that do little more than drain budgets and clutter desks.

That feeling of frustration—watching your competitors stand out while your efforts seem invisible. The disappointment of seeing your brand's potential wasted on products that don't create lasting impressions. The nagging fear that you're missing something, that others know a secret you don't.

Here's what most don't realise—promotional merchandise isn't about just slapping a logo on a product and hoping for the best. It's about strategy, psychology, and precision. Every successful campaign is built on a deep understanding of what makes people engage, remember, and take action.

And now with the possibility of tighter marketing budgets and rising competition, the margin for error is shrinking fast. Every pound spent on branding must work harder than ever before. There's no room for guesswork.

It seems most are left in a state of doubt—constantly second-guessing their choices, watching their competitors thrive while they struggle to see any tangible results. The fear of irrelevance creeps in. The worry that their brand will never truly stand out. And worst of all, the sinking realisation that if they don't crack this soon, they'll keep wasting money, missing opportunities, and falling further behind.

The Profitless Promotion Trap

You're stuck. Spinning your wheels. Pouring money, time, and effort into trying to make your brand stand out—yet nothing seems to stick. You've tried everything. Or so you think. But instead of creating powerful, lasting connections with your audience, you're trapped in an endless cycle of wasted resources, fleeting engagement, and diminishing returns.

This is the Profitless Promotion Trap—a five-step loop of frustration that countless business owners, marketers, and sales professionals find themselves caught in. No matter how many times you go through it, you always end up right back at the start, wondering where it all went wrong.

Let's walk through it, step by painful step.

1. The Desperate Search

Maybe your latest marketing campaign fell flat. Perhaps your sales team is struggling to get prospects to remember your brand. Or maybe you're watching competitors effortlessly attract and retain customers while you're stuck treading water.

Whatever the case, you know one thing for sure—you need something different. Something that makes people notice you, remember you, and choose you over everyone else.

So, you start searching. You look at what others are doing. You Google marketing trends. You scroll through social media, read articles, maybe even ask colleagues for advice. There are so many options, so many possible solutions, and yet... nothing feels quite right.

Pressure mounts. A deadline looms. You don't have time to overthink it. You just need to take action. Which leads you to the next step...

2. The Quick Fix

You make a decision. Maybe it's based on a trend you saw online. Maybe it's what a competitor is doing. Or maybe it's just what's available and easy to execute. Whatever it is, you commit. You invest. You tell yourself, This is it. This is going to work.

Momentum kicks in. You roll out your campaign, send out your materials, launch your promotion. You feel relief, even a little excitement—finally, you're doing something.

And then... nothing.

No buzz. No lasting engagement. Maybe a few polite acknowledgements, a handful of likes, a short-lived spike in interest—but then it all fades, just as quickly as it began.

Which brings you to the next stage...

3. The Deafening Silence

Days pass. Weeks, even. You check your numbers, your sales, your engagement. You wait for the impact to hit.

But it doesn't.

Customers aren't talking about you. No one remembers what you did. Your brand is no stronger than it was before. And worst of all? You're starting to realise that all that money, time, and effort was for nothing.

Doubt creeps in. Frustration builds. You start second-guessing yourself. Maybe it was the wrong choice. Maybe we didn't execute it properly. Maybe we just didn't spend enough.

And then, the worst thought of all: Maybe nothing works.

But you can't afford to give up. You need results. So, you do what seems like the only logical thing...

4. The Justification Phase

You convince yourself that you weren't entirely wrong. Maybe the timing was off. Perhaps the execution could have been better. Or maybe you just need to try a different spin on the same idea.

So, you tweak your approach. You refine the message. You make small adjustments, thinking this time, it'll be different. You justify spending more money because this time it will work.

You tell yourself that success is just around the corner. That next time will be the breakthrough. That you're so close.

And with renewed determination, you take the leap again...

5. The Fleeting Hope

At first, it feels like you were right. There's a small spike in engagement. Your team feels optimistic. Maybe a few customers respond positively. You breathe a sigh of relief.

This time, it's working.

Until it isn't.

The excitement dies down. The response fizzles out. The results are no better than before. And now, you're not just frustrated— you're exhausted.

You start seeing the pattern. The same cycle, over and over again. And yet, somehow, you've ended up right back where you started... searching for a way to finally make your brand stand out.

And so, the loop begins again.

—-

It just goes to show—you would be wise to do something different if you truly want to create memorable brand experiences that attract and retain clients, differentiate your business from competitors, and achieve a high return on investment. You need a strategy that works. A system that breaks this cycle once and for all.

Which is why I'm glad you're reading this book. Because as you turn the page and start reading, you will finally get the answers and insight you've been looking for.

INTRODUCTION

Promotional merchandise is everywhere. Branded pens, tote bags, water bottles, T-shirts—you name it. Companies spend billions on giveaways, yet most of it ends up in the bin, forgotten in a drawer, or worse, completely ignored.

Why?

Because most businesses get it wrong. They treat merch like an afterthought. A cheap add-on. A box to tick. But when done right, promotional merchandise isn't just swag—it's a strategic weapon. It builds brand loyalty, sparks conversations, and drives real sales.

You've seen brands that nail it. Their merch isn't just something people take—it's something they want. It's worn, displayed, and shared. It becomes a status symbol, a talking point, even a source of revenue.

That's the difference between junk and genius. And the good news? You don't need a billion-dollar budget to get it right.

THE REAL REASON MOST PROMOTIONAL MERCH FAILS

Most businesses throw money at promotional products without

a plan. They pick something cheap, slap a logo on it, and hope for the best.

That's like throwing darts blindfolded.

The result?

- Pens that run out of ink in a week.
- T-shirts that end up as pyjamas (or worse, dust rags).
- Plastic keychains that no one asked for.
- Notebooks that gather dust in a drawer.

No impact. No engagement. No return on investment.

The biggest mistake? Choosing products without thinking about who will actually use them. What do they need? What would they love to have? What fits seamlessly into their life?

The best brands don't just give things away—they create experiences. Their merch isn't just functional; it's desirable. It's something people want to keep, use, and show off. And when they do, the brand stays top of mind.

If you've ever felt like your promotional products weren't working, you're not alone. But the problem isn't the concept— it's the execution.

THE POWER OF MERCH THAT ACTUALLY WORKS

The right merch does more than just put your logo in someone's hands. It creates an emotional connection. It taps into psychology—how people remember brands, how they value gifts, and how they associate meaning with objects.

Think about the last time you got a freebie that you actually loved. Maybe it was a premium water bottle that became your daily go-to. A soft, perfectly fitting hoodie that you wore everywhere. A sleek notebook that made you feel more organised.

Every time you used it, you thought about the brand behind it. And over time, that brand became familiar, trusted, even preferred.

That's the power of great merch.

It lives in your customer's world. It becomes part of their routine. It sparks conversations.

And when done right, it does something even more powerful—it drives action.

- It makes people want to engage with your brand.
- It turns casual customers into loyal advocates.
- It boosts sales, not just awareness.

WHY THIS MATTERS MORE THAN EVER

In a world drowning in digital ads, physical merchandise stands out.

Think about how many ads you scroll past in a day. How many

emails you delete without reading. How many times you skip a YouTube ad the second you can.

Now think about the impact of something tangible. A beautifully designed product that lands directly in a customer's hands. No algorithms. No competition for attention. Just a direct, personal brand experience.

That's why smart businesses are doubling down on merch.

It cuts through the noise. It creates a lasting impression. And when paired with the right strategy, it turns passive audiences into active buyers.

This isn't about handing out random freebies and hoping for the best. It's about using promotional merchandise as a tool—one that builds your brand, engages your audience, and drives real revenue.

If you've ever wondered how some brands turn simple swag into cult-like followings, how they make people line up for limited-edition drops, or how they use merch to create lifelong customers, you're in the right place.

This is how you do it right.

1

WHY MOST PROMOTIONAL MERCHANDISE FAILS (AND HOW TO GET IT RIGHT)

"The bitterness of poor quality remains long after the sweetness of low price is forgotten." — Benjamin Franklin

The Common Pitfalls That Waste Money

Choosing the Wrong Products

If you've ever walked away from a conference with a flimsy pen that stops working within a week or a key chain that ends up in a drawer, you already know what bad promotional merchandise feels like. It's forgettable at best and a waste of money at worst. The problem? Too many companies choose swag based on cost, convenience, or impulse rather than strategy.

You've seen it before—businesses ordering bulk quantities of generic mugs, stress balls, or cheap tote bags with their logo slapped on. These items don't add value to the recipient's life. They don't create an emotional connection. Instead, they end up in a bin, left behind in hotel rooms, or stuffed in a junk drawer, never to be thought of again.

The key mistake here is selecting merchandise based on what is cheap or easy to order rather than what aligns with your brand and customer needs. If your swag doesn't have a purpose or a place in your audience's daily life, it's dead on arrival.

High-quality, functional merchandise has staying power. A durable, stylish water bottle, a power bank, or a well-designed notebook will be used repeatedly, keeping your brand in front of your customer for months, even years. Instead of looking for the least expensive option, consider what your ideal customer actually wants to use.

Lack of Strategy

Promotional merchandise isn't just something you hand out at events or throw into a shipping box as an afterthought. When done right, it's a marketing tool that can increase brand awareness, build customer loyalty, and drive actual sales. But too often, businesses treat swag as an extra rather than a strategic investment.

Without a plan, most promotional products are just random giveaways. They lack a clear objective and fail to support broader marketing efforts. What's the goal? Are you trying to generate leads, increase social media engagement, or reward loyal customers? Every piece of merchandise should serve a specific purpose.

Think about the best promo items you've received—ones you've actually kept and used. Now, consider why you still have them. Was it something useful? Was it high-quality? Did it come at the right time? That's the level of thought you need to put into your promotional merchandise strategy.

Every item should be tied to a clear marketing goal. For example:

- If you want to boost lead generation, offer a high-value item in exchange for email sign-ups.
- If your focus is brand recall, invest in quality products that customers will use daily, like apparel or tech accessories.
- If you're aiming to increase customer retention, create exclusive, limited-edition merch for repeat buyers.

Without strategy, you're just handing out stuff. With strategy, you're building a brand experience.

Ignoring Your Audience

Not every customer wants the same type of merchandise. A fitness brand handing out plastic desk toys isn't just off-brand— it's a missed opportunity. Your audience determines what kind of merch will work and what will be a complete waste.

Demographics play a role. A Gen Z audience might appreciate stylish, eco-friendly tote bags or reusable water bottles, while a corporate B2B audience might prefer sleek notebooks or premium pens. Psychographics go even deeper—what are their interests, habits, and daily routines? If you align your merchandise with their lifestyle, they'll not only use it but also associate your brand with something positive.

Here's where most businesses fail: they choose products based on what they like rather than what their customers want. You might think a branded USB drive is useful, but if your audience is cloud-based and mobile-first, they'll never use it. Likewise, if you're marketing to executives, a cheap plastic pen won't impress them—it'll make your brand look second-rate.

The best way to avoid this mistake? Listen to your audience. Look at customer data, conduct surveys, and analyse past campaigns. If a previous merch item didn't perform well, don't repeat the same mistake. Find out what your customers actually want and give them something they'll love to use.

If your merchandise doesn't fit your audience's lifestyle, it won't just be ignored—it'll actively hurt your brand perception.

The Psychology Behind Promotional Merchandise

What if I told you a single, well-designed promotional product could make your brand unforgettable? Not just "Oh yeah, I think I've heard of them" memorable—but top-of-mind, emotionally connected, and impossible to ignore memorable. The secret isn't just in the product itself; it's in the psychology behind it.

Handing out branded merchandise isn't about slapping your

logo on something cheap and hoping people remember you. It's about understanding why people keep, use, and emotionally connect with certain items—and leveraging that knowledge to drive real business results.

The Power of Reciprocity

You know that warm, fuzzy feeling when someone gives you something unexpectedly? That's the power of reciprocity in action. It's one of the most powerful psychological triggers in marketing.

The principle is simple: when someone receives something of value—especially when they didn't have to—it creates an internal pressure to return the favour. Whether they realise it or not, they feel the need to reciprocate in some way.

Ever noticed how restaurants give mints along with the bill? Studies show that when a waiter adds a small, unexpected gift (like a mint or chocolate), tips increase by up to 23%. That's reciprocity at work.

Now, apply this to promotional merchandise. If you give someone a high-quality, useful, or emotionally resonant item without asking for anything in return, they instinctively feel compelled to return the favour in some way—whether that's engaging with your brand, following you on social media, or even making a purchase.

The key is perceived value. A cheap plastic pen won't trigger the same effect as a premium notebook, a sleek water bottle, or a beautifully designed T-shirt that actually fits well. When the gift feels intentional and valuable, the recipient is more likely to reciprocate with loyalty, engagement, or even advocacy.

Use this to your advantage:

- **Make it personal** – If possible, personalise the item with their name or something unique to them.
- **Deliver it unexpectedly** – A surprise gift has more impact than one they expect.
- **Give without immediate expectation** – The moment it feels transactional, it loses its psychological power.

People want to reciprocate generosity. Give them something worth remembering, and they'll return the favour in ways you can't predict.

Emotional Connection with Brands

Think about the last time you felt genuinely attached to a brand. Maybe it was your favourite coffee shop, a clothing brand that just gets your style, or a tech company whose products you swear by. What made them stand out?

Chances are, it wasn't just their logo or marketing—it was how they made you feel.

Emotional connection is the foundation of brand loyalty, and promotional merchandise plays a surprisingly powerful role in fostering it. The right product can create an experience—a daily reminder of your brand that sparks positive emotions.

Here's how it works:

- **Tactile memory** – When people physically interact with an object repeatedly (like a favourite mug or notebook), they form an emotional bond with it.
- **Association with positive experiences** – If your merch is given in a meaningful context (like a VIP event, a heartfelt thank-you, or a milestone celebration), it holds sentimental value.
- **Identity reinforcement** – People love products that align with their identity. If your merch reflects their values, interests, or aspirations, it strengthens their connection to your brand.

Ever noticed how people love branded tote bags from high-end brands? It's not about the bag—it's about what it represents. Owning and using it signals something about their identity.

The goal isn't just to put your logo on an item—it's to create something that people feel proud to use.

How to build emotional connection through merch:

- **Tap into personal identity** – Create items that align with your audience's lifestyle, values, and aspirations.
- **Make it part of a meaningful moment** – Give away merch during experiences that evoke emotion (celebrations, milestones, exclusive events).
- **Think beyond the product** – The packaging, the way it's presented, and the story behind it all contribute to the emotional impact.

7

If you can make someone feel something when they use your merch, you've won more than just a branding opportunity—you've created a loyal advocate.

How Memory Influences Buying Decisions

Your brain is a fascinating (and sometimes lazy) machine. It loves shortcuts. One of the biggest shortcuts it takes is relying on familiarity when making decisions.

Think about supermarket shelves. You're standing in front of 20 different brands of coffee. Which one do you grab? Chances are, it's the one you recognise. Not necessarily the best one. Not even the cheapest one. Just the one your brain has seen before and tagged as "safe."

That's the power of repeated exposure. And promotional merchandise is one of the best ways to hack it.

Every time someone sees, touches, or uses your merch, it reinforces brand recognition. Over time, this familiarity turns into preference. It's called the mere exposure effect—the more we're exposed to something, the more we like and trust it.

Imagine two competing businesses trying to win over the same customer. One sends an email. The other sends a beautifully designed, high-quality notebook that sits on the customer's desk for months. Who's more likely to be remembered when it's time to buy?

Merchandise keeps your brand physically present in people's

8

lives—not just as a fleeting ad or email, but as a tangible object they interact with daily. That's why it's so effective.

How to make memory work in your favour:

- **Choose high-use items** – The more often someone inter-acts with your merch, the stronger the memory reinforce-ment.
- **Make your branding subtle but recognisable** – If it looks too much like an advertisement, people may ditch it. Aim for seamless integration into their lives.
- **Be consistent** – Repetition builds recognition. If you use merch strategically and consistently, your brand becomes the obvious choice when they're ready to buy.

When done right, promotional merchandise isn't just a giveaway—it's a memory hack. It keeps your brand at the forefront of your customers' minds without them even realising it.

Promotional merchandise isn't just about slapping your logo on a product and hoping for the best. It's about tapping into deep psychological principles—reciprocity, emotional connection, and memory—to create something far more powerful than a simple freebie. When you understand how the human brain interacts with branded products, you can transform your merch from forgettable junk into an invaluable marketing asset.

Setting the Foundation for Success

9

Defining Clear Objectives

Promotional merchandise without a clear objective is like throwing darts blindfolded. You might hit something, but it won't be what you aimed for. Before you even think about ordering that batch of branded water bottles or custom tote bags, you need to get brutally specific about what you want them to achieve.

Are you trying to generate leads? Strengthen brand recall? Encourage repeat business? Each goal demands a different approach. A giveaway at a trade show won't serve the same purpose as a high-end client appreciation gift. A freebie in an online order is not the same as merchandise designed to create viral social media buzz.

The mistake most businesses make is assuming that all promo items should drive direct sales. That's not how this game works. Promotional merchandise is a tool to enhance engagement, build relationships, and create brand stickiness. Sales come as a by-product of well-executed strategy.

Start by asking three questions:

1. **What is the primary outcome I want?** (Brand awareness, customer retention, lead generation, etc.)
2. **How will I measure success?** (New leads collected, social media mentions, repeat purchase rates, etc.)
3. **How does this merchandise fit into my overall marketing strategy?**

If you can't answer these questions clearly, you're not ready to invest in promotional merchandise yet. Clarity here prevents wasted budget and ensures everything you create has a purpose.

Aligning with Brand Identity

Your promotional merchandise should feel like an extension of your brand, not an afterthought. Too many businesses slap a logo onto whatever's cheapest and hope for the best. That's why their merch ends up stuffed in a drawer or, worse, in the bin.

Every item you choose should reflect your brand's personality, values, and positioning. If you're a luxury brand, handing out flimsy plastic pens is a disconnect. If sustainability is a core part of your messaging, your merchandise should be eco-friendly. If you're in tech, your merch should feel modern and innovative.

Think of brands that have nailed this. Apple doesn't give out random promotional junk. Their merch is sleek, minimalist, and premium—just like their products. Red Bull's branded gear reflects their high-energy, extreme sports-driven identity. The merch reinforces the brand rather than diluting it.

Your promotional items should pass the "Would I actually use this?" test. If it feels cheap, uninspired, or irrelevant to your brand, don't waste your money. Instead, focus on products that seamlessly fit into your audience's lifestyle while reinforcing your brand message.

Understanding Customer Desire

Most businesses think about promotional merchandise from their own perspective—what's affordable, what's easy to produce, what fits within their branding guidelines. That's completely backwards. The key to effective merchandise is understanding what your customers actually want.

People don't care about your brand as much as you do. They care about what benefits them. Your merchandise should align with their needs, interests, and daily routines.

A few key questions to consider:

- **What would my ideal customer find genuinely useful?**
- **What type of merchandise would they actually carry, wear, or use regularly?**
- **What would make them excited to receive and share this with others?**

For example, if you're targeting busy professionals, high-quality notebooks, sleek tech accessories, or premium coffee tumblers might be a perfect fit. If you're appealing to a younger, fashion-conscious audience, trendy apparel, limited-edition streetwear, or aesthetic water bottles could be the way to go.

The more your merchandise integrates into your customers' daily lives, the more brand impressions you generate. A tote bag used for grocery shopping, a phone stand on a work desk, or a gym water bottle that gets carried everywhere—these are all walking billboards for your brand.

The best promotional merchandise makes the recipient feel like they've received something valuable, not just another throw-away freebie. That's the difference between being remembered and being forgotten.

2

STRATEGIC THINKING – HOW TO CHOOSE MERCH THAT WORKS

"Quality is never an accident; it is always the result of intelligent effort."
— John Ruskin

The Science of Product Selection

Promotional merchandise is more than just slapping a logo on a random object and hoping it does something useful for your brand. The right product can turn a casual customer into a loyal advocate. The wrong one? It ends up in a bin, forgotten before it even had a chance to make an impact. You need to be strategic. There's a science to picking the right merchandise, and it starts with understanding utility, durability, and relevance.

Utility vs Novelty

There's a reason people keep certain promotional items and discard others. You'll rarely see someone excited about another flimsy plastic pen, but a high-quality water bottle or a well-designed tote bag? That's different. The difference lies in utility—how often and how effectively someone can use your product in their daily life.

When choosing merchandise, ask yourself: Would I personally use this? Would I pay for this if it wasn't free? If the answer is no, rethink your choice.

Novelty items—quirky, fun, or unique products—can work, but they need to be relevant to your brand and audience. A tech company handing out fidget spinners might feel outdated now, but a custom-branded wireless charger? That's useful. Novelty only works when it has relevance.

The best approach is to blend utility with novelty. A product that's both useful and has an element of fun or uniqueness sticks in people's minds. Think about a branded notebook with an innovative layout that helps with productivity, or a reusable coffee cup with a sleek design. These are items that people not only keep but also use regularly, reinforcing your brand every time they do.

Durability and Perceived Value

A cheap pen that stops working after two days does more harm than good. You don't want your brand associated with something that feels disposable. Durability matters because the longer an item lasts, the longer your brand stays in front of your customer.

Consider the difference between a flimsy plastic key chain and a well-made leather one. The former gets tossed in a drawer; the latter stays on a keyring for years. When you choose products that are built to last, they create a perception of quality that extends to your brand. You're not just giving away an item— you're reinforcing your reputation.

Perceived value also plays a massive role. A £1 promotional item that looks and feels premium can have a stronger impact than a £5 item that feels cheap. Customers don't always know the actual cost, but they can feel quality. A product with a little weight, a smooth finish, or a sleek design naturally feels more valuable.

If you're working with a tight budget, focus on fewer high-quality items rather than mass-producing cheap throwaways. It's better to give away 100 premium notebooks that customers love than 1,000 plastic trinkets that end up in landfill.

Trends vs Timelessness

Trendy merchandise can give your brand a fresh, modern feel, but trends also fade. The challenge is knowing when to ride a trend and when to stick to timeless essentials.

For example, five years ago, PopSockets were everywhere. Brands that jumped on the trend early saw great engagement. But today? Many people have moved on. On the other hand, classic promotional items like reusable drinkware, tote bags, and tech accessories have remained relevant for years.

So, what's the right approach? A mix of both.

Timeless items ensure longevity—things like high-quality notebooks, well-made pens, insulated bottles, and premium tote bags never go out of style. Meanwhile, trend-based items can create buzz and excitement, especially when used for limited-time campaigns. If a new trend aligns with your brand and resonates with your audience, it can be worth testing.

A great strategy is to modernise timeless items. Instead of a generic tote bag, offer a stylish, foldable one made of sustainable materials. Instead of a basic USB drive, try a sleek, branded power bank. You get the longevity of a classic product with the excitement of a fresh design.

The key to picking the right merchandise isn't just about what's popular or what's cheap—it's about choosing items that people actually want to use. The more useful, durable, and relevant your merch is, the stronger the connection people will have with

17

your brand.

Matching Merchandise to Your Ideal Customer

Demographics vs Psychographics

Trying to sell to everyone is a guaranteed way to sell to no one. The same applies to promotional merchandise. If you don't know exactly who you're targeting, you'll end up with a pile of unsold, unused, or thrown-away products.

Demographics are the basics—age, gender, income, location. They're useful for broad strokes but won't tell you why someone would actually care about what you're giving them. That's where psychographics come in. Psychographics dig into attitudes, interests, and behaviours. They reveal how people think, what they value, and what makes them take action.

For example, if you're marketing to tech-savvy professionals, a branded leather notebook might be a waste of money. They're probably already hooked on digital note-taking apps. A high-quality wireless charger? Now you're speaking their language. On the other hand, if your audience is made up of fitness enthusiasts, a branded yoga mat or stainless-steel water bottle will get daily use and keep your brand front and centre.

The key is to go beyond surface-level assumptions. Just because someone is in their 40s doesn't mean they want a golf towel. Just because they work in finance doesn't mean they want another cheap pen. Look at what they actually do, what they care about, and what products seamlessly integrate into their lives.

Start by asking:

- **What does my ideal customer do every day?**
- **What do they already carry with them?**
- **What would they genuinely find useful?**

If you can answer these questions, you'll never waste money on throwaway merch again.

Lifestyle Integration

The best promotional merchandise doesn't sit in a drawer. It becomes part of someone's daily routine. If your merch ends up buried in the back of a cupboard or tossed in the bin, it's useless. You need to think about how your product fits into your customer's lifestyle so that your brand stays visible and relevant.

Look at how the biggest brands approach this. Apple doesn't give away cheap plastic keychains; they create sleek, functional accessories that fit seamlessly into their customers' tech-driven lives. Starbucks doesn't hand out flimsy paper notebooks; they offer reusable cups that coffee lovers actually use.

Your merchandise should feel like an extension of your customer's habits. If your audience is made up of remote workers, a well-designed laptop stand or noise-cancelling earbuds could be a hit. If they travel frequently, a high-quality travel pouch or RFID-blocking wallet makes sense.

Think about where your product will live. Will it sit on a desk, be carried in a bag, or be used outdoors? If you can embed your brand into someone's daily routine, you're not just giving away merch—you're earning long-term brand exposure.

A good way to test this is to ask yourself, "Would I actually use this?" If the answer is no, don't expect your customer to either.

Creating Emotional Resonance

People don't just use products; they connect with them. The best promotional merchandise doesn't just serve a function—it triggers an emotion. If you can tap into nostalgia, exclusivity, or personal identity, your merch will hold meaning beyond just being another branded item.

Exclusivity is a powerful tool. If something feels rare or limited, people will want it more. A standard branded tote bag might get ignored, but a limited edition tote designed by a well-known artist? That suddenly has value.

Nostalgia also plays a huge role in emotional attachment. Think about the resurgence of retro-style products—cassette tapes, vintage tees, classic gaming merch. If you can create a connection to a shared cultural moment, your merchandise will carry extra weight.

Personal identity is another major factor. People love products that align with their values and self-image. If your audience is passionate about sustainability, a reusable bamboo cutlery set will resonate far more than a generic plastic giveaway. If they're hardcore gamers, a custom-designed mechanical keyboard keycap could become a prized possession.

Merch isn't just about slapping a logo on something and calling it a day. It's about creating something that people actually want to own, use, and talk about. If your product sparks an emotional reaction, it won't just get used—it'll get shared, talked about, and remembered.

The Budgeting Equation – ROI Over Cost

Calculating Lifetime Value

Spending money on promotional merchandise without understanding its financial impact is like throwing darts blindfolded. You might hit the target, but most of the time, you'll miss. To make sure every pound you invest in branded merch pulls its weight, you need to think beyond the upfront cost. The real question isn't, "How much does this cost?" but rather, "What's the long-term return?"

This is where Customer Lifetime Value (CLV) comes in. If you know how much a customer is worth over their entire relationship with your brand, you can justify spending more on high-quality merchandise that creates a stronger connection.

Let's say your average customer spends £500 per year with you and stays loyal for five years. That's a CLV of £2,500. Would you hesitate to spend £10 or even £20 on a well-crafted promotional item that helps secure that loyalty? Probably not.

The mistake most businesses make is focusing on one-time

transactions instead of long-term relationships. A cheap, forgettable giveaway might cost less in the moment, but if it does nothing to reinforce your brand or create an emotional bond, it's wasted money. On the other hand, a well-thought-out, high-quality item that becomes part of your customer's daily life keeps your brand front and centre for years.

A branded notebook that someone uses daily, a premium insulated water bottle they take everywhere, or even a sleek, well-designed tech gadget—these aren't just freebies. They're brand touchpoints. Every time they're used, your brand gets another moment of attention.

To maximise CLV with merchandise, ask yourself:

- **Does this item create a repeated interaction with my brand?**
- **Will my ideal customer actually use this?**
- **Does this reinforce our brand's quality and values?**

If the answer to any of these is no, rethink your choice.

Balancing Quality & Affordability

There's a dangerous misconception that spending less is always better when it comes to promotional merchandise. The reality? Cutting costs too much often leads to cheap, disposable junk that does nothing for your brand. People don't remember who gave them a flimsy plastic pen that broke in a week. But they do remember the brand that gave them a premium leather-bound notebook they actually enjoy using.

The key is finding the sweet spot between quality and affordability. You don't need to break the bank, but you do need to ensure that whatever you give out reflects the value of your brand.

A few rules to follow:

- **If it feels cheap, it makes your brand look cheap**. People subconsciously associate the quality of a freebie with the quality of your company.
- **Longevity matters.** A high-quality product that lasts for years is a better investment than a throwaway item that gets binned in days.
- **Functional beats flashy.** A well-designed, useful product will always outperform a gimmicky item that gets a quick laugh but no long-term use.

Instead of spreading your budget too thin, consider fewer, better-quality items for a more targeted audience. A premium, thoughtfully chosen product given to 100 key prospects will outperform 1,000 forgettable giveaways handed out at random.

If your budget is tight, think strategically. Consider bundling your merchandise with a purchase instead of handing it out for free. Or use it as an incentive for referrals, ensuring that each piece of merch helps generate revenue.

The goal isn't just to give something away—it's to create an impact.

Measuring Cost per Impression

Throwing money at promotional merchandise without tracking its effectiveness is a fast way to waste your budget. A smarter approach is treating it like any other marketing investment—by measuring its impact.

One of the best metrics to track is Cost Per Impression (CPI). This tells you how much you're paying for each time your brand is seen or noticed through your merchandise.

Here's how it works:

1. **Calculate the total cost of your merchandise campaign.**
2. **Estimate how many times your branded item will be seen over its lifespan.**
3. **Divide the total cost by the estimated impressions.**

For example, if you spend £5,000 on 1,000 premium branded water bottles, and each bottle is used daily for a year, getting seen by an average of two people per day, that's:

1,000 bottles ×365 days ×2 impressions per day = 730,000 impressions

Now, divide the total cost:

£5,000 ÷730,000 = £0.006 per impression

That's less than a penny per impression—far cheaper than digital ads, which often cost £1 or more per click with no guarantee of long-term brand recall.

Compare this to a low-quality plastic pen that costs £0.50 but is used only once and thrown away. If it gets three impressions before landing in the bin, your CPI is £0.17 per impression—28 times higher than the water bottle.

Quality merchandise doesn't just last longer—it keeps working for you long after the initial investment.

To take it further, QR codes or unique discount codes can help track direct conversions from your merchandise. If a branded item drives a customer to visit your website, sign up for an email list, or make a purchase, you can quantify its direct impact on revenue.

The bottom line? Promotional merchandise isn't an expense—it's an investment. When chosen strategically, high-quality branded products generate impressions, build brand affinity, and drive repeat business for a fraction of what you'd pay in traditional advertising.

3

DESIGN LIKE A MARKETING GENIUS – CREATING MERCH PEOPLE WANT TO KEEP

"Design is not just what it looks like and feels like.
Design is how it works."
– Steve Jobs

Branding That Sticks

Think about the last promotional item you actually kept. Not the cheap plastic pen that ran out of ink after a week, or the flimsy tote bag that ripped after two uses. The ones that stayed in your life had something more – they looked good, felt good, and, most importantly, they didn't scream "free corporate junk."

Branded merchandise isn't just about slapping your logo on a product and hoping for the best. It's about embedding your brand into something people actually want to use. The right design ensures your merch doesn't end up in a drawer or, worse, the bin. Done correctly, it transforms a simple giveaway into a brand touchpoint that sticks in people's minds (and hands) for years.

Logos vs Subtle Branding

Your logo is important, but it's not the star of the show – the product is. The best promotional merchandise doesn't feel like an advertisement; it feels like a product someone would buy for themselves.

A massive, in-your-face logo on a t-shirt or a mug makes it feel like a billboard. The result? People won't wear or use it unless they have to. Instead, think about brands like Apple or Supreme. Their logos are minimal, discreet, and, in some cases, entirely absent. Yet, their products are instantly recognisable because of their design language.

Consider alternative branding techniques:

- **Small, well-placed logos** – A subtle mark on the sleeve of a premium hoodie instead of a giant centre-chest print.
- **Iconography over logos** – A unique symbol or visual element related to your brand that people associate with you.
- **Branded patterns** – A repeat pattern featuring elements of your brand subtly incorporated into the design.

Minimal branding makes your merch feel like a stylish product rather than a corporate giveaway. When people wear or use it, they do it because they like it – not because they feel obligated.

Colour Psychology

Colour isn't just about aesthetics; it influences perception, mood, and even purchasing decisions. Some of the biggest brands in the world have mastered colour psychology to reinforce their identity. Coca-Cola's red evokes excitement and passion, while Tiffany's blue screams exclusivity and luxury.

When choosing colours for your merchandise, ask yourself:

- **Does this align with my brand's personality?** If your brand stands for sustainability and calmness, neon green might not be the best choice.
- **Does it work in real life?** A bright orange hoodie might look great in theory, but will people actually wear it?
- **How does it stand against competitors?** If everyone in your industry is using blue, a bold yellow might help you stand out.

You don't need to stick rigidly to your brand colours, but they should be a reference point. A muted or tonal variation of your brand's palette can make the product more wearable while still reinforcing who you are.

Typography and Readability

Text on merch can be tricky. If it's too small, it's unreadable. If it's too large, it looks cheap. If it's in the wrong font, it's forgotten.

Typography should be clean, legible, and suited to the product.

Some key guidelines:

- **Avoid overly decorative fonts** – Script or novelty fonts might look fun, but they can be hard to read, especially from a distance.
- **Think about context** – A bold, all-caps sans-serif might be great for a gym brand but feel aggressive for a wellness company.
- **Size matters** – Text should be large enough to be read easily but not so big that it dominates the design.

A simple, well-thought-out phrase in the right font can make all the difference. Branded t-shirts that people actually wear often feature short, catchy slogans in clean typography rather than oversized company names.

When your promotional merch is designed with intention, it moves beyond being a throwaway item. It becomes a product people not only keep but actively want to use.

Visual Appeal and Functionality

Promotional merchandise that people actually want to use isn't just about slapping a logo on a random product. It needs to look good, feel good, and serve a purpose. A beautiful product that's useless will get tossed. A useful product that looks terrible will get buried in a drawer. The sweet spot is where aesthetics and utility meet—where form and function work together to create something people actually want to integrate into their lives.

Minimalism vs Bold Designs

Every brand has a personality, and your merchandise needs to reflect it without overwhelming the person receiving it. Some brands thrive on minimalist, sleek designs—think Apple's clean aesthetic or Muji's understated simplicity. Others benefit from loud, bold visuals—like Red Bull's high-energy branding or Supreme's iconic, in-your-face logo placements.

If your brand leans towards premium, luxury, or sophisticated, a minimalist approach works best. A beautifully embossed logo on a high-quality notebook, a subtle engraving on a stainless steel bottle, or a monochrome tote bag with a sleek design can make a lasting impression. Less is more when you're aiming for class and elegance.

On the other hand, if your brand is all about excitement, fun, or making a statement, bold designs can work wonders. Bright colours, oversized logos, and unique patterns grab attention instantly. Think of merchandise like vibrant socks with quirky prints, neon-branded sunglasses, or oversized hoodies with striking graphics.

The key is knowing what fits your brand's identity. A law firm handing out neon green hats with massive logos? Probably not great. A streetwear brand doing the same? Perfect. Your merchandise should feel like a natural extension of your brand, not a desperate attempt to be noticed.

Texture and Material Choices

A product's feel can be just as important as how it looks. People associate textures with quality—cheap plastic feels cheap, while soft-touch matte finishes, premium fabrics, and high-end metals create a perception of value.

Think of the difference between a flimsy plastic pen and a smooth, weighty metal one. The latter immediately feels more expensive, even if it only costs a little more to produce. The same goes for apparel—cheap, stiff cotton t-shirts don't get worn, while soft, high-quality cotton or moisture-wicking fabric makes people want to keep using them.

Materials also play a role in sustainability, and people are paying attention. Recycled fabrics, bamboo products, and biodegradable packaging aren't just environmentally friendly— they also elevate your brand's image. A reusable water bottle made from recycled stainless steel sends a stronger message than a cheap plastic one.

Texture matters in unexpected ways too. A notebook with a leather-like soft-touch cover feels premium. A tote bag with a canvas finish instead of a thin polyester one feels sturdy and worth keeping. A branded hoodie with a fleece interior feels luxurious. When selecting merchandise, always think about how it will feel in the user's hands or on their body.

Custom vs Generic Products

Customisation separates throwaway merchandise from brand-building assets. Generic products—off-the-shelf mugs, pens, and t-shirts with a basic logo—are forgettable. They don't create an emotional connection. Custom products, however, feel intentional and valuable.

Consider the difference between a basic white mug with your logo slapped on it and a ceramic mug with a unique shape, a custom interior colour, and an embossed logo. The latter feels like something people would actually buy. It transforms a generic giveaway into a branded experience.

The same principle applies across all merchandise. A tote bag with a clever, industry-related phrase instead of just a logo becomes something people want to carry. A water bottle with a motivational quote relevant to your audience (rather than just your company name) feels like a personal touch.

This also extends to packaging. A product that comes in a beautifully designed box—even if it's simple—immediately feels more valuable. Unboxing is an experience, and when you elevate that experience, your brand stays memorable. Even small details, like adding a handwritten note or using recyclable wrapping, create an impression that lasts beyond the initial interaction.

When you combine aesthetics with functionality, you create merchandise that isn't just promotional—it's desirable.

Creating a "Must-Have" Factor

Limited Edition & Exclusivity

Scarcity creates demand. It's why luxury brands thrive, why people queue overnight for the latest trainer drop, and why limited-edition promotional merchandise can turn casual brand interactions into fanatical loyalty. When an item is available only for a short time, it triggers urgency. No one wants to miss out.

The trick is positioning your promotional merch so it feels exclusive, not just another freebie. Limited runs of high-quality goods—whether it's apparel, drinkware, or something completely unique to your brand—instantly increase perceived value. A t-shirt that's available all year loses its appeal. A t-shirt tied to an event, campaign, or milestone with a fixed number available? That's something people will chase.

Numbering items adds another level of desirability. If you're giving away 500 custom notebooks, consider marking them "1 of 500," "2 of 500," and so on. This simple detail transforms an ordinary giveaway into something people treasure.

Another approach is time-sensitive exclusivity. Offer merchandise only to those who take action within a specific window—whether they're signing up for a webinar, making a purchase, or attending an event. The scarcity effect kicks in, and people act faster when they know the opportunity won't last.

VIP-only merchandise also taps into exclusivity. Reward loyal customers, top-tier clients, or engaged community members with special edition items that aren't available to the public. When your audience feels like they're part of an inner circle, they'll go to great lengths to stay there.

Collectible Series

Humans are wired to complete sets. It's why people collect trading cards, stamp books, and even fast-food toys. When promotional merchandise is designed as part of a series, it creates a natural incentive for people to engage repeatedly with your brand.

A great strategy is releasing items in waves. Instead of handing out the same branded mug at every event, create a series with different designs, themes, or messages. Attendees who received the first in the series will be motivated to return for the next one.

This works exceptionally well for tech companies, fitness brands, and lifestyle businesses. If you run a conference annually, create a new edition of your merch each year— something that event regulars will want to collect. If your brand has a strong community presence, consider a quarterly or seasonal drop that keeps customers engaged throughout the year.

Gamification also drives collectibility. If customers need to complete a challenge, attend multiple events, or reach certain spending levels to collect all pieces of a set, they'll stay engaged far longer than they would for a single giveaway. This is the strategy behind loyalty cards where customers collect stamps for rewards—it works because of the psychological need to finish what's been started.

Even simple variations on a core product can create a sense of collectibility. A brand that gives away reusable tote bags might design a new version each year with different artwork or slogans. Loyal customers will want to collect them all.

Personalisation & Customisation

People value things more when they feel personally connected to them. Generic promotional items fade into the background, but when someone receives something tailored specifically to them, it becomes instantly more meaningful.

Names are the easiest way to create this connection. A water bottle with a generic logo is just another freebie. A water bottle with your customer's name engraved on it? That's something they'll use daily. Many companies now leverage variable printing or laser engraving to personalise merch at scale. Even something as simple as allowing customers to add their initials to an item boosts retention rates significantly.

Beyond names, giving people the ability to customise their merch creates an even stronger bond. Offer choices in colours, designs, or messaging. If you're giving away t-shirts, let people pick from multiple designs instead of handing out the same one to everyone. When people get a say in what they receive, they're far more likely to keep and use it.

Interactive personalisation goes even further. QR codes that link to a custom message, user-generated content printed onto merchandise, or even merch that changes based on customer preferences all enhance engagement. A well-known example of this is Coca-Cola's "Share a Coke" campaign, where bottles featured common names. People hunted for their names or those of their friends, creating a viral effect.

The key is making customers feel like the item was made just for them. Whether it's a name, a design they chose, or an item that reflects their interests, personalised merchandise isn't just another freebie—it's something they'll want to keep.

4

INTERMISSION – A SMALL ASK WITH A BIG IMPACT

"We all need people who will give us feedback. That's how me improve."
– Bill Gates

Would you help a fellow business owner, marketer, or sales professional if it took less than a minute?

If so, we have a quick request—one that costs you nothing but has the power to help someone just like you.

Somewhere out there, a business owner is struggling to break through the noise. A marketer is searching for fresh ways to engage customers. A sales professional is looking for that edge to close more deals. And right now, they have no idea that the strategies in this book could be the game-changer they need.

That's where you come in.

Most people judge a book by its ratings and reviews. They skim the comments, searching for a reason to take the next step. Your honest review could be the reason they decide to invest in their brand, sharpen their strategy, and finally see real results.

If this book has given you value so far, would you take 60 seconds to leave a quick review?

Here's how to do it:

- If you're on Kindle, scroll to the bottom of the book and swipe up—Amazon will prompt you to leave a review.
- If you're on Audible, tap the three dots in the top right corner and select 'Rate & Review.'
- If you're reading a physical copy, head to the book's page on Amazon, scroll down, and click 'Write a Customer Review.'

Your review isn't just a rating—it's a beacon for someone looking for answers. It helps them take action, avoid common pitfalls, and build a brand that stands out.

We appreciate you taking the time to do this. And now, back to building Merch That Works for you.

5

WHERE & WHEN TO USE PROMOTIONAL MERCH FOR MAXIMUM IMPACT

"The aim of marketing is to know and understand the customer so well the product or service fits them and sells itself." — Peter Drucker

TRADE SHOWS AND EVENTS

Trade shows and events are a battleground. A sea of booths, flashing lights, and endless giveaways. Most companies show up, dump a pile of cheap pens and stress balls on a table, and hope for the best. That's not a strategy—it's a waste of time and money. You need to be intentional about how you use merch at events, or you'll get drowned out by the noise.

Standing Out in a Sea of Freebies

Your competitors are handing out the same generic swag—tote bags, keychains, and flimsy water bottles. Attendees grab them out of habit, not excitement. By the end of the day, most of it ends up in a hotel rubbish bin or buried under a pile of brochures. If your merch isn't memorable, it's useless.

The goal isn't just to give something away—it's to create an experience. You want attendees to stop, engage, and remember you long after they leave. The best way to do that? Give them something they actually want.

- **Make it exclusive.** Instead of dumping merch on a table, make people earn it. Maybe they have to scan a QR code, follow your social media, or sit through a quick demo. When something isn't handed out like candy, it feels more valuable.
- **Make it interactive.** A lucky draw, a spin-the-wheel game, or a live customisation station can turn merchandise into an attraction instead of an afterthought.
- **Make it premium.** If your merch is cheap and forgettable, your brand will feel the same way. High-quality items— wireless chargers, insulated tumblers, or branded note- books with real leather covers—send a message that you care about quality.

Look at the tech giants. Apple doesn't hand out plastic pens at events. They give away sleek, beautifully designed swag that people want to use. Your promotional merch should reflect your brand's value, not undermine it.

Driving Foot Traffic

At a crowded event, getting people to your booth is half the battle. You can't afford to sit back and hope attendees wander over. You need to create a reason for them to stop.

- **Use merch as a beacon.** Attendees talk. If they see someone carrying an incredible branded item, they'll ask, "Where did you get that?" Make your merch desirable enough that people actively seek out your booth.
- **Leverage FOMO.** Announce limited-time giveaways at specific hours. "First 50 visitors at 2 PM get an exclusive merch bundle" creates urgency and crowds.
- **Turn it into a social moment.** Set up an Instagram-worthy display with your best merch and encourage attendees to take photos. Require them to tag your brand to claim their giveaway. Free exposure and foot traffic in one move.

Think about the psychology behind this. People want to feel like they've discovered something cool, not just been handed another throwaway item. Create a sense of exclusivity, and attendees will do the marketing for you.

Post-Event Follow-Up Strategies

Most companies fail at the follow-up. They spend thousands on trade shows, collect a stack of business cards, and then... silence. Your merch should be the beginning of the relationship, not the end.

- **Turn merch into a conversation starter.** Include a call-

41

to-action with your giveaway. A QR code that leads to a personalised landing page, a discount code for event attendees—something that keeps the interaction going beyond the event.

· **Send a secondary gift.** If you had meaningful conversations with high-value prospects, send them a follow-up package. A handwritten note with a premium piece of branded merch (like a high-end notebook or wireless speaker) makes you stand out in their inbox.

· **Track engagement.** Use unique codes or customised URLs on your giveaways to see how many attendees actually take action. If no one is engaging, you know your merch wasn't memorable enough.

Trade shows and events aren't just about showing up—they're about making an impact. Most companies treat promotional merchandise as an afterthought. You can use it as a strategic tool to attract attention, create engagement, and build lasting relationships.

Direct Mail Campaigns Done Right

Adding a Physical Touch to Digital Marketing

Digital marketing is saturated. Your audience is bombarded with emails, ads, and social media posts all day. Most of it gets ignored, deleted, or scrolled past without a second thought. But when something physical lands in their hands—something they can touch, hold, and use—it cuts through the noise in a way that digital never can.

Direct mail is far from obsolete. When done strategically, it's a powerhouse for engagement and brand recall. The key is making sure your promotional merchandise isn't just another piece of junk mail that ends up in the bin. It has to provide value, create an experience, and leave a lasting impression.

Start by thinking about what would grab your attention if it arrived at your doorstep. A generic pen with a logo? Probably not. A high-quality notebook with a personalised note? That's a different story. The goal is to send something that feels intentional, useful, and worth keeping.

Tactile experiences leave deeper imprints in memory than digital interactions. When people physically engage with an object—whether it's unboxing, using, or even just feeling the texture—it strengthens brand recall. A well-thought-out promotional item keeps your brand in their hands and, more importantly, in their mind.

Brands that understand this leverage the power of tangible marketing to complement their digital efforts. Instead of just sending another email, they include a QR code on a premium merch item that leads to an exclusive landing page or discount. Instead of cold outreach via LinkedIn, they send a personalised package that sparks curiosity and opens doors for conversation.

Surprise & Delight Factor

Most mail is either bills or junk. That's why an unexpected package stands out immediately. Done right, direct mail creates a moment of surprise and delight—an emotional response that strengthens brand affinity and increases the likelihood of engagement.

The secret is in the unexpected element. If your recipient is used to receiving dull corporate mail, sending them something personal and high-quality shifts their perception of your brand. A simple but elegant branded mug in premium packaging feels like a gift rather than an advertisement. A custom-engraved keyring with their initials shows attention to detail. These small gestures matter more than you think.

Timing plays a huge role here. Sending an item right after a key interaction—like a new customer signing up, a prospect taking a demo, or a high-value lead engaging with your campaign—maximises impact. If someone just attended your webinar, sending them a follow-up package with a thoughtful, related gift makes your brand unforgettable.

Adding a personal touch amplifies the effect. A handwritten note, a custom message, or even referencing something specific about the recipient makes your outreach feel intentional rather than mass-produced. Personalisation turns an ordinary promo item into a meaningful brand experience.

The best brands create anticipation around their mailers. They tease it in emails or social media, drop hints, or even use mystery packaging to build intrigue. When people are excited to open your package rather than seeing it as just another piece of mail, you've already won half the battle.

Crafting the Perfect Mail Package

It's not just about what you send; it's how you send it. Packaging matters. The way an item is presented influences perception and perceived value. A high-quality product in a cheap plastic envelope loses its impact. But the same product in a well-designed, branded box with thoughtful wrapping elevates the entire experience.

Think about unboxing. People love the experience of opening something special. That's why high-end brands invest in packaging that feels premium. A well-packaged promotional item makes your brand feel more valuable.

Here's what makes a direct mail package stand out:

· **A strong first impression:** Use high-quality packaging that feels like an experience to open. Even something as simple as a matte black box with your logo in foil print can make a statement.
· **A clear, engaging message:** Include a note or card that explains why they're receiving this package. This isn't just about thanking them—it's about reinforcing your brand message and encouraging the next step.
· **A call to action:** What do you want them to do next? Scan a QR code? Visit a landing page? Use a discount code? Make it clear and easy. - A genuinely useful or desirable promo item: If it's cheap, generic, or irrelevant, it won't stick. Choose something that fits your brand and provides real value to the recipient.

Well-executed direct mail creates a ripple effect. Recipients talk about it, share it on social media, and even show it to colleagues. When done well, it's not just a marketing effort—it's a conversation starter that keeps your brand top of mind.

Employee and Client Gifting Strategies

Turning Employees into Brand Ambassadors

Your employees are your first and most powerful brand ambassadors. They live and breathe your company culture, interact with customers, and shape the public perception of your business. If you're not equipping them with high-quality, well-designed promotional merchandise, you're missing out on a massive opportunity.

The key is to make sure the merch you give them is something they actually want to wear or use. No one wants to be a walking billboard for a company they work for if the branding is obnoxious or the product feels cheap. The goal is to create merchandise that makes them feel valued and part of something bigger.

Start with apparel. A well-fitted, stylish hoodie, jacket, or T-shirt with a subtle logo—something they'd actually wear outside of work—turns them into walking endorsements for your brand. The same goes for high-quality backpacks, water bottles, or tech accessories. If it's something they'd buy themselves, you've nailed it.

Another way to make employees feel valued is through exclusive, employee-only merchandise. Limited-edition gear, reserved just for your team, adds an element of exclusivity that makes them feel recognised. It also reinforces a sense of belonging. Think of brands like Google or Apple—employees proudly wear company-branded jackets or carry branded gear because it signifies they're part of something special.

You can also turn employee gifting into an experience. Instead of just handing out swag, create a moment around it. Maybe it's a welcome kit for new hires with a premium notebook, a sleek pen, and a high-quality mug. Or a milestone gift for work anniversaries—something meaningful and practical, like a customised duffle bag or noise-cancelling headphones. The more thought you put into it, the more they'll appreciate it and use it.

Encourage organic promotion by making it easy for employees to share their merch on social media. A well-designed onboarding kit or an exclusive piece of swag for hitting a milestone is something they'll want to show off. Attach a hashtag, create a little internal competition, and you've got an army of brand ambassadors spreading your name without even thinking about it.

Strengthening Client Relationships

Clients don't remember emails. They remember experiences. And the right promotional merchandise can turn a simple business transaction into a long-term relationship.

The trick is to give them something they'll use—something that integrates into their daily life while keeping you top of mind. A cheap pen or a random keychain isn't going to cut it. You want thoughtful, high-quality items that feel personal and valuable.

Start with practical, premium gifts. Wireless chargers, sleek notebooks, insulated drinkware—items that fit seamlessly into their workflow or lifestyle. If your client is always on the go, a high-end travel mug or a durable power bank makes sense. If they're in an office setting, a minimalist desk organiser or a high-quality leather notebook is something they'll appreciate and use regularly.

Personalisation takes it to the next level. A generic branded item is fine, but adding their name, initials, or a small customised touch makes it feel like it was made just for them. A leather notebook embossed with their name or a premium pen with a subtle engraving transforms a simple gift into something meaningful.

Timing also plays a huge role in client gifting. Surprise them when they least expect it. A thoughtful, well-timed gift—whether it's after closing a deal, following a successful project, or just as a thank-you—goes a long way in strengthening the relationship. It shows appreciation without an immediate sales agenda attached.

Presentation matters just as much as the gift itself. A beautifully packaged, well-thought-out gift creates an experience. A handwritten note adds an extra touch. Don't just ship them a branded water bottle in a plain box—create an unboxing experience that makes them feel valued.

Don't underestimate the power of exclusivity. Limited-edition, VIP-only merchandise can create a sense of appreciation and status. Maybe it's an invite-only, high-end merchandise pack for your top-tier clients or an annual collector's item that they look forward to receiving. If it feels special, they'll associate that feeling with your brand.

Holiday & Milestone Gifts

Holidays and milestones are prime opportunities to strengthen relationships with both employees and clients. A well-thought-out gift during these moments isn't just a nice gesture—it's a strategic move that keeps you at the forefront of their mind in the best way possible.

The mistake most businesses make is going generic. A cheap pre-packaged fruit basket? Forgettable. A standard corporate calendar? Straight to the bin. The goal is to give something that feels intentional, useful, and aligned with your brand.

For employees, holiday gifts should feel like a reward, not an afterthought. A curated gift box with high-quality snacks, premium coffee, or a unique experience-based gift (like an online class or subscription) makes them feel appreciated. If you want to go the branded route, think stylish winter apparel—beanies, scarves, or a well-designed fleece jacket they'd actually want to wear.

Milestone gifts should celebrate achievements, whether it's a work anniversary, a promotion, or hitting a big goal. A personalised gift—like a custom leather bag, premium wireless earbuds, or even an experience like a dinner voucher—can make a lasting impact. The more tailored it is to the individual, the stronger the impression.

For clients, holiday gifting is an opportunity to stand out from the sea of generic corporate gifts they receive. Instead of the classic wine-and-cheese basket they've seen a hundred times, go for something unique and high-end. A bespoke cocktail kit, a set of premium artisanal chocolates, or a beautifully designed coffee table book relevant to their industry can set you apart.

If your brand has a sustainability focus, eco-friendly gift options can reinforce that message. Reusable coffee cups, high-quality tote bags, or stylish bamboo office accessories align with a socially responsible brand image while still being practical and valuable.

Presentation is everything. A well-packaged, beautifully wrapped gift with a personal note instantly elevates the experience. It turns a simple item into an emotional touchpoint. It's not just about the gift—it's about how it makes them feel when they receive it.

6

THE SECRET SAUCE – HOW TO MAKE MERCH DRIVE REAL SALES

"People don't buy what you do; they buy why you do it."
— Simon Sinek

Using Scarcity and Urgency

When something is rare, people want it more. When time is running out, they act faster. Scarcity and urgency aren't just sales gimmicks—they're deeply rooted in human psychology. They create demand, drive action, and turn ordinary promotional merchandise into powerful brand assets that generate real revenue. Big brands use these tactics to sell out limited-edition trainers, exclusive event tickets, and seasonal product drops. You can apply the same principles with your merch strategy to increase engagement, boost sales, and make your brand unforgettable.

Limited-Time Giveaways

A freebie is great, but a freebie with an expiration date? That's a lead magnet with teeth. When you set a deadline on availability, you create urgency. People hate missing out—it's why flash sales work, why concert tickets sell out in minutes, and why limited-time promotions drive spikes in engagement.

Instead of handing out promotional merchandise whenever and to whoever, tie it to an event, a campaign, or a deadline. For example:

- Offer an exclusive branded item only to the first 100 people who sign up for a webinar.
- Create a 48-hour giveaway for customers who purchase during a specific launch window.
- Use a countdown timer on your website for a merch bundle only available for a few days.

The key is to make the opportunity feel special. When people realise they can't get your merch anytime they want, they'll feel compelled to grab it while they can. And once they have it, they'll associate that sense of urgency with your brand, making them more likely to engage with future campaigns.

VIP-Only Access

Not all merch should be available to everyone. When you create an exclusive tier of access, you increase perceived value and strengthen customer loyalty. People love feeling like insiders— like they're part of an elite club with special privileges. When you position your merchandise as something only available to your best customers, top clients, or event attendees, you create demand simply by making it scarce.

Take a cue from major brands that use VIP access to drive engagement:

- Apple gives staff-only branded T-shirts, making them sought-after collector's items.
- Luxury brands release invitation-only merchandise for their top-tier customers.
- Tech companies create conference-exclusive swag only available to attendees.

You can apply this to your own business by offering merch as a reward for top-tier customers, long-term clients, or high-value referrals. When people see others getting something they can't have, they'll work harder to gain access. It's simple psychology—people want what they can't easily get.

A few ideas:

- Send VIP-branded gifts to your most loyal customers, making them feel valued.
- Offer an exclusive merch drop only to your email subscribers or social media followers.
- Create a "members-only" collection of promotional items that can't be bought—only earned.

The goal is to make your merchandise feel like a privilege, not just a giveaway. When you do this right, your customers won't just want your merch—they'll crave it.

Countdown Campaigns

A ticking clock is one of the most effective sales tools you have. When time is running out, hesitation disappears. That's why countdown timers work so well in marketing—they create urgency, force decision-making, and push people to take action before it's too late.

You can apply this same principle to your promotional merchandise by running countdown campaigns tied to sales, events, or product launches. Here's how:

- **Pre-launch exclusives** – Offer a limited-edition product only available for pre-orders before a certain date.
- **Seasonal drops** – Release special merch tied to holidays or seasons, only available for a short time.
- **Time-sensitive rewards** – Give customers a free branded item if they purchase within a specific window.

Use countdown timers on your website, email campaigns, and social media to reinforce the urgency. The more visible the deadline, the more effective it will be.

A great example of this in action? Black Friday deals. Every year, brands generate billions in sales simply by limiting offers to a short timeframe. The same principle applies to your merch strategy. When people see a countdown, they act—because the fear of missing out is stronger than the desire to wait.

By combining scarcity and urgency in your promotional mer-chandise campaigns, you turn passive interest into active en-gagement. People will chase your merch, not just accept it. And when that happens, your brand isn't just giving away merchandise—it's building demand.

Creating a Referral and Loyalty System

Rewarding Word-of-Mouth

Your best salespeople aren't on your payroll. They're your customers. The ones who rave about your product, drop your name in conversations, and convince their friends to buy from you. A strong referral system fuels this natural behaviour. The goal is to make your customers feel like insiders—rewarded for sharing your brand, but in a way that feels organic, not transactional.

The key is to integrate promotional merchandise into the referral process in a way that feels exclusive and desirable. Generic freebies won't cut it. You need to create something that people actually want to earn.

A tiered system works well. For example:

- **Refer one friend** – Get an exclusive branded item (not for sale, only available through referrals).
- **Refer three friends** – Get a premium version of the item (higher value, more desirable).
- **Refer five friends** – Get a limited-edition bundle or an experience (VIP access, event invites, etc.).

55

The psychology here is simple: people value what they can't easily get. If your merchandise is only available through referrals, it instantly becomes more desirable. That's why companies like Tesla and Dropbox have thrived on word-of-mouth marketing—they reward their advocates with status, exclusivity, and perks that money can't buy.

Another way to drive referrals is through a social-sharing incentive. Let's say you're launching a new product. Offer a high-quality branded item to customers who share their purchase on social media, tag your brand, and get engagement (likes/comments). You're turning your customers into micro-influencers, spreading your brand for you while giving them something valuable in return.

The mistake many brands make? Giving away cheap, forgettable swag as a referral reward. If the reward isn't worth talking about, the referral programme will fail. Your merchandise needs to have real perceived value—something your audience would actually be excited to receive.

Tiered Loyalty Incentives

Loyalty isn't bought. It's earned. The best loyalty programmes don't just reward purchases; they create an emotional connection between the customer and the brand. The goal isn't just to get repeat sales—it's to build a tribe of customers who wouldn't dream of going anywhere else.

Merchandise plays a critical role in this. A well-designed loyalty system uses branded products to acknowledge milestones, celebrate engagement, and make customers feel valued beyond the transaction.

A tiered system keeps people engaged. Consider structuring something like this:

- **Entry-Level (First Purchase)** – A small but thoughtful branded item. Example: A high-quality sticker pack, enamel pin, or reusable tote bag.
- **Mid-Tier (Multiple Purchases or Spend Threshold)** – A functional, everyday-use item that integrates with their lifestyle. Example: A premium water bottle, notebook, or tech accessory.
- **VIP Tier (High Spend or Long-Term Loyalty)** – Something exclusive, limited-edition, or customisable. Example: A branded jacket, luxury pen, or personalised travel bag.

The secret to making this work? The rewards must feel progressive. If your first-tier reward is a cheap keychain and your final-tier reward is another cheap keychain, what's the motivation to keep going? Each level needs to feel like an upgrade.

Subscription-based businesses have used this brilliantly. Take a brand like YETI—their loyalty programme offers exclusive, high-quality branded gear at different milestones, reinforcing their premium positioning. Customers don't just buy a YETI product; they become part of the YETI ecosystem.

The same principle applies whether you're running an e-commerce store, a SaaS business, or a service-based brand. The goal is to give customers a reason to keep engaging, not just to keep buying. Branded merchandise should be a symbol of their relationship with you—a badge of honour that signifies they're part of something valuable.

Surprise Freebies That Keep Customers Hooked

Predictability kills excitement. When customers know exactly what to expect, engagement drops. That's why the best loyalty and retention strategies build in an element of surprise. Unexpected gifts create a sense of delight—something that makes people feel valued and acknowledged.

The key is to make it feel personal. A random freebie in the mail has more impact than a predictable discount code. Done right, an unexpected piece of merch can turn a one-time buyer into a lifelong fan.

Consider these strategies:

- **"Just Because" Gifts** – Send out limited-edition branded merchandise to top customers with no explanation other than "We appreciate you." Example: A high-quality mug with an inside joke or reference that resonates with your audience.
- **Anniversary Rewards** – Celebrate the one-year mark of a customer's first purchase with exclusive merch. Example: A branded hoodie or a premium notebook with a handwritten thank-you note.
- **Social Media Interactions** – If a customer posts about your brand frequently, surprise them with a gift. Example: A custom piece of merch with their name on it, sent as a thank-

you for their engagement.

A legendary example is Zappos. They're known for sending unexpected gifts to customers—anything from free upgraded shipping to handwritten notes and surprise swag. This kind of generosity builds loyalty in a way that no discount code ever could.

Another way to use surprise merchandise is through gamifica-tion. Let's say you have an e-commerce store. Instead of just offering a discount for every X amount spent, introduce a mys-tery merch reward. Customers don't know what they'll get until they hit the threshold—triggering curiosity and excitement.

Spotify did this brilliantly with their Wrapped campaign. Every year, they send out personalised data insights and occasionally surprise top users with exclusive gifts (branded items, posters, even physical mixtapes). The result? Customers feel special, and they share their experience widely—creating organic brand advocacy.

The goal here isn't just to give away free stuff—it's to create memorable moments. A well-placed, unexpected piece of merch makes people feel valued, which in turn makes them more likely to stay engaged with your brand.

Loyalty isn't about points and discounts. It's about making customers feel like they belong. When you use high-quality, well-thought-out merchandise as a tool for engagement—not just a giveaway—you build something far more valuable than repeat sales. You build a community.

Leveraging Influencers and Brand Advocates

Identifying the Right Partners

Not all influencers are created equal, and partnering with the wrong one is like throwing money into a fire. It doesn't matter how many followers they have if those followers aren't your target audience. You need relevance over reach.

Start by defining who your ideal customer listens to. This isn't always the mega-influencers with millions of followers. In fact, micro-influencers (those with 10,000 to 100,000 followers) often have a much more engaged audience. Their followers trust them because they feel accessible, relatable, and authentic.

Look at engagement rates—comments, shares, and real conversations—not just likes. A 500,000-follower influencer with a 1% engagement rate is far less valuable than a 50,000-follower influencer with a 10% engagement rate.

Once you've shortlisted potential partners, research their past collaborations. Do they actually use and believe in the products they promote? If they're constantly switching brand allegiances, their audience will see straight through it. You want someone who aligns with your values, who would naturally use your merchandise in their everyday life.

When reaching out, don't just send a generic pitch. Make it personal. Show them you've done your homework. Highlight why your brand fits their audience and propose a mutually beneficial collaboration. Some influencers prefer paid partnerships, while others are happy with free products if they genuinely love them. Either way, the relationship should feel like a natural extension of their personal brand.

Establish clear expectations. What kind of content will they create? How many posts? Will they do unboxings, tutorials, or giveaways? Ensure you have a structured agreement that protects both sides. If the partnership feels forced or overly scripted, their audience will disengage, and the promotion will fall flat.

Co-Branded Merchandise

Aligning with the right influencer or brand advocate doesn't have to stop at a one-off post. Co-branded merchandise is a powerful way to create something exclusive that benefits both parties.

Think of it as a fusion of your brand and their identity— something their audience wants to own. The key is to make it feel special rather than a generic promo item. It could be a custom design, a unique colourway, or a limited-edition run only available through them.

A successful example of co-branded merchandise is Nike's collaborations with athletes and designers. Limited-edition trainers sell out in minutes, not because they're just another pair of trainers, but because they carry the identity of the person or brand they're linked to.

Now, you don't need to be Nike to make this work. A coffee brand could partner with a fitness influencer to create a co-branded insulated travel mug. A marketing agency could collaborate with a business coach to produce a sleek, minimalist notebook for entrepreneurs. The possibilities are endless, but the key is to make it unique and aligned with both identities.

The exclusivity factor is what makes it valuable. If it's just another branded T-shirt or pen, no one cares. But if it's a collaboration that people associate with someone they admire, it becomes desirable.

The best way to distribute co-branded merch is through limited drops. Announce it with your influencer partner, create hype, and make it clear that once it's gone, it's gone. This not only creates demand but also drives urgency—people don't want to miss out on something they know won't be restocked.

Encouraging User-Generated Content

The real magic happens when your customers and followers start creating content about your merchandise without being asked. This is how you turn promotional merch into a viral marketing tool.

People love showing off cool swag—especially if it makes them look good or aligns with their personal brand. The trick is to make your merch shareable. It should be something they want to post on their Instagram story, TikTok, or LinkedIn.

Think about unboxing experiences. If your packaging is high-quality, sleek, or comes with a personalised note, people will be more inclined to share it. Plain, unbranded boxes are a missed opportunity. Invest in packaging that adds to the experience.

Create a branded hashtag and encourage people to use it when posting. Feature user-generated content on your own channels. When people see others engaging, they'll want to be part of the movement.

Run contests where customers post pictures with your merch for a chance to win something exclusive. It could be early access to a new product, a VIP experience, or even just more cool merch. The key is to incentivise participation in a way that feels fun rather than forced.

Another powerful strategy is to include a call to action with your merchandise. A simple card inside the package that says, "Tag us in a photo for a chance to be featured" can work wonders. It's a small nudge that encourages people to engage.

The most successful brands don't just give out merch—they create experiences around it. If your merch is something people are proud to show off, it will naturally spread across social media, giving you free publicity and strengthening brand loyalty.

7

DISTRIBUTION STRATEGIES – GETTING MERCH INTO THE RIGHT HANDS

"The secret of success in business is to know something
that nobody else knows."
– Aristotle Onassis

IN-PERSON VS DIGITAL DISTRIBUTION

Giving away promotional merchandise is easy. Getting it into the right hands at the right time, in a way that actually generates sales and brand loyalty? That's a different game entirely. Too many businesses treat merch distribution like an afterthought— tossing out freebies at events or stuffing random swag into online orders without any real strategy. That's just burning money. You need a plan that ensures your merchandise isn't just received but appreciated, used, and remembered. The key decision: are you going to distribute in person or digitally? Each approach has its strengths, and choosing wisely can mean the difference between wasted effort and real brand impact.

Event Giveaways vs Online Exclusives

Handing out promotional merchandise in person lets you control the experience. You get to see the reaction, create a moment, and tie the giveaway to a conversation or relationship. This is why event giveaways remain one of the most powerful ways to distribute merch. But there's a right way and a wrong way to approach it.

The wrong way? Dumping a pile of cheap pens or stress balls on a table and hoping people grab them. This does nothing for your brand. The right way? Making your merch part of a memorable interaction. If you're at a trade show, don't just hand out a tote bag—make it a "VIP" bag only available to those who engage with your booth in a meaningful way. If you're hosting a seminar, give attendees something they'll actually use, like a high-quality notebook with subtle branding.

Online exclusives, on the other hand, allow you to be more selective. Instead of giving away merch to anyone who walks by, you can target the right people. A well-placed "free gift with purchase" offer can increase conversion rates significantly. A limited-edition product available only to email subscribers can drive sign-ups. A branded hoodie offered as a reward for loyal customers can strengthen retention.

The trick is to make the merch feel special. If anyone can get it, it's just another freebie. If it's exclusive—available only to certain customers, at certain times, or in limited quantities—it becomes desirable.

Packaging and Unboxing Experience

Most businesses focus only on what they're giving away. Few think about how it's presented. That's a mistake because the way you package and deliver your merchandise can be just as important as the item itself.

Take Apple, for example. Their packaging is an experience—clean, minimalist, premium. People don't just open an iPhone box; they savour the process. Your promotional merch should aim for the same effect.

If you're handing out merch in person, don't just shove it into someone's hand. Present it. Use a sleek bag with your branding, or wrap the item in tissue paper with a personalised note. If you're shipping merch, make the unboxing experience feel premium. A well-designed box, a thank-you card, and careful presentation can turn an ordinary freebie into something people talk about.

And don't underestimate the power of surprise. Adding an unexpected piece of merch to an order—something the customer didn't know they were getting—creates a moment of delight. That moment translates into social media shares, word-of-mouth marketing, and repeat business.

Tracking Distribution Effectiveness

If you can't measure it, you can't improve it. Most businesses have no idea if their promotional merchandise is actually working because they don't track distribution properly. They give away products, cross their fingers, and hope for the best. That's not a strategy.

Start by setting clear goals for your merch distribution. Are you using it to generate leads? Drive sales? Increase brand awareness? The goal determines the metric you should track.

For in-person giveaways, track engagement. How many people took action after receiving your merch? Did they visit your website, sign up for a demo, or make a purchase? QR codes, unique discount codes, or custom landing pages can help you measure this.

For online distribution, track redemption rates. If you're offering a free gift with purchase, how many people are taking advantage of it? If you're using merch to drive email sign-ups, how many new leads are coming in?

Don't just look at immediate results. The real power of promotional merchandise is in its long-term impact. A high-quality item that stays in use keeps your brand top-of-mind for months, even years. Survey customers to find out if they're still using your merch. Check social media for organic mentions. Look at repeat purchase rates among customers who received merchandise versus those who didn't.

By treating merch distribution as a strategic investment rather than a random giveaway, you can turn what most businesses see as a cost into a powerful revenue-generating tool.

Leveraging E-commerce and Subscription Models

Bundling with Purchases

People love getting something extra. When done right, bundling promotional merchandise with purchases can increase average order value, boost customer retention, and make your brand more memorable. The key is to ensure the merch adds real perceived value—no one gets excited about a flimsy keyring tossed in as an afterthought.

Think about your best-selling products or services. What complementary merchandise would enhance the experience? A high-end coffee brand could bundle stylish reusable mugs with bulk bean orders. A fitness equipment company could include branded resistance bands with purchases over a certain amount.

Scarcity plays a role here. Limited-time bundles create urgency and drive conversion rates. If customers know a premium-branded tote is only available for the next 500 orders, they're more likely to act now rather than wait.

Another strategy is tiered bundling. Offer different levels of freebies based on spending thresholds. For example:

- **Spend £50** → Get a branded notebook.
- **Spend £100** → Get a premium water bottle.

· **Spend £200** → Get an exclusive hoodie.

This encourages customers to add more to their cart to unlock the next tier. You're not just increasing sales—you're making your brand a part of their lifestyle.

Merch as an Upsell

Upselling works when it feels natural and enhances the customer's experience. A well-placed, well-designed piece of merchandise can be the nudge that pushes a customer to spend more.

Let's say you run an online store selling high-end tech accessories. A customer is checking out with a £120 pair of noise-cancelling headphones. Right before they complete the purchase, they see an option to add a branded travel case for a discounted price. It's not just a random add-on—it's something relevant, useful, and aligned with their purchase.

The trick is to position the merch as an exclusive opportunity rather than an afterthought. "Upgrade your order and get our limited-edition branded carry case for 30% off" sounds compelling. "Would you like to add a case?" feels like an annoying pop-up.

Subscription businesses can take this even further. If you run a subscription box service, offering exclusive branded merch as an upsell between renewals can increase retention. Maybe your meal kit service includes a premium apron for subscribers who commit to a six-month plan. Or your SaaS company offers a branded notebook for annual subscribers instead of monthly ones.

Upselling isn't about squeezing more money out of customers—it's about providing extra value in a way that makes saying "yes" easy.

Subscription Box Strategies

Branded merch fits seamlessly into the subscription model because it creates anticipation and excitement. When done right, it can increase customer lifetime value and turn subscribers into long-term brand advocates.

The first strategy is integrating exclusive branded items into the monthly or quarterly subscription box experience. If you run a beauty subscription service, adding a high-quality branded cosmetics bag once a year makes your package feel more premium. A coffee subscription could include a branded travel cup in the winter months. These aren't random freebies—they enhance the product experience and strengthen brand affinity.

A second approach is offering a merch-only subscription. Think of how major brands like Nike and Adidas roll out exclusive clothing drops to their most loyal customers. A niche brand could do something similar with limited-edition branded apparel, drinkware, or accessories. The key is exclusivity—subscribers should feel like they're getting something special that isn't available elsewhere.

A third strategy is using branded merchandise as a retention tool. One of the biggest challenges in the subscription business is churn—customers cancelling after a few months. Offering milestone rewards can keep them engaged. A branded hoodie after six months. A personalised notebook after a year. A VIP-only merch item for long-term subscribers. These small incentives can be the difference between a customer sticking around or dropping off.

Subscription models thrive on engagement, and branded merchandise is one of the easiest ways to turn passive customers into loyal fans. It's not just about slapping your logo on random items—it's about creating a tangible connection between your brand and customers that keeps them coming back.

Using Merch for Lead Generation

Getting your promotional merchandise into the right hands isn't just about brand awareness—it should be bringing in leads, warming up potential customers, and driving sales. The right merch, when used strategically, turns cold prospects into engaged buyers. This isn't about handing out freebies and hoping for the best. It's about designing a system where every piece of merch works as a lead magnet, pulling potential customers into your ecosystem.

Freebies That Capture Emails

Handing out free stuff without a plan is just throwing money away. If you're giving away promotional items without capturing customer data, you're missing a massive opportunity. Every piece of merch should have a purpose, and in lead generation, that purpose is to get contact details.

Start by making the exchange clear: no one gets the freebie without giving something in return. This could be an email address, a social media follow, or even a survey response. The key is making the process seamless—no one wants to fill out a six-field form just to get a branded pen.

Here are some ways to turn merch into a lead capture tool:

- **Exclusive Giveaways:** Set up a landing page where people can enter their email to claim a free item. This works well for hot-ticket merch, like limited-edition apparel or high-quality drinkware.
- **Trade Show Booths:** Instead of dumping promo items on a table, require attendees to scan a QR code and enter their details before they get their free gift.
- **Social Media Contests:** "Tag a friend and drop your email to enter" creates both engagement and a lead database.
- **Event Check-Ins:** Use merch as an incentive for people to register in advance or check in at your event.

The merch itself should be desirable enough that people are willing to give up their email or social handle to get it. If it's just another cheap tote bag, they'll pass. But a high-quality, sleek notebook or a stylish insulated bottle? That's worth typing in an email address.

Don't stop at just collecting emails. Follow up. Send a thank-you email immediately with a discount code or exclusive content to reinforce their interest. If you disappear after the freebie, so will they.

Gamification & Contests

People love games, and they love winning. When you add a competitive element to your merch strategy, you create urgency, excitement, and, more importantly, a reason for people to engage with your brand.

One of the easiest ways to gamify merch is through tiered giveaways. Instead of giving away the same item to everyone, create different levels of rewards based on engagement.

For example:

· **Sign up for our newsletter** → Get a sticker pack.
· **Refer a friend** → Get a branded mug.
· **Make a purchase** → Get an exclusive hoodie.

This keeps people engaged and motivates them to take additional actions beyond just handing over their email.

Spin-to-win wheels, scratch-off cards, and digital raffles are also effective. If you've ever seen people line up at a trade show to spin a prize wheel, you already know how powerful this tactic is. The suspense of winning something, even if it's small, is enough to draw people in.

Social media also makes gamification easy. Run a "comment to win" contest where users tag friends and engage with your brand. Or take it further by encouraging user-generated content, like posting a selfie with your merch for a chance to win a bigger prize.

The key is to make participation effortless. If people have to jump through hoops, they won't bother. Keep the process as simple as possible while still capturing leads and engagement.

Turning Cold Leads into Warm Prospects

Promotional merchandise shouldn't end at lead capture—it should move people down your sales funnel. A freebie gets you in the door, but the real magic happens when you use that merch to spark engagement and nudge leads toward conversion.

One of the most effective ways to do this is through follow-up sequences. Once someone claims their free merch, they should immediately enter a well-designed email or SMS sequence that nurtures them toward a sale.

Here's how you can structure it:

1. **Immediate confirmation:** "Thanks for claiming your free gift! It's on the way—while you wait, here's 10% off your first purchase."
2. **Engagement email:** A few days later, send a message that adds value, like a how-to guide or customer story related to your product.
3. **Social proof:** Another email showcasing testimonials or user-generated content featuring your merch.
4. **Exclusive offer:** A limited-time discount or VIP offer to push them toward making a purchase.

If you're using QR codes or NFC technology in your merch, take advantage of it. A well-placed code on a water bottle or notebook can link straight to a landing page with a special offer. It's a seamless way to turn a physical giveaway into a digital conversion.

Another underused tactic is personalisation at scale. If you collect any data at lead capture—like job title, industry, or interests—use it to tailor follow-ups. A generic "thanks for signing up" email is forgettable, but a personalised message referencing their specific industry makes an impression.

Lastly, use merch to open conversations. If you're at an event, don't just hand someone a T-shirt and walk away. Use it as a conversation starter—"We made these for our best customers. What do you do?" This shifts the interaction from transactional to relational, which is where real sales happen.

Promotional merchandise isn't just about brand visibility. Used correctly, it's a powerful tool for lead generation, audience engagement, and customer conversion. If you're just giving things away without a plan, you're missing the real opportunity—turning that freebie into future revenue.

8

TESTING, TRACKING & MEASURING ROI ON PROMOTIONAL MERCHANDISE

"What gets measured gets managed."
— Peter Drucker

SETTING UP KEY METRICS FOR SUCCESS

If you're not tracking the return on investment (ROI) of your promotional merchandise, you're flying blind. Too many businesses throw money at branded merchandise without understanding whether it's actually driving results. You wouldn't run a paid ad campaign without measuring conversions, so why treat promotional products any differently?

The key is to set up clear metrics before you even place your first order. You need to know what success looks like, how you'll measure it, and what levers you can pull to improve performance. Let's break it down.

Cost per Acquisition vs Cost per Impression

Most businesses default to tracking cost per unit—how much each promotional item costs to produce and distribute. But that number alone tells you nothing about effectiveness. Instead, you need to focus on two critical metrics: cost per acquisition (CPA) and cost per impression (CPI).

Cost per Acquisition (CPA) is the amount you spend on merchandise to acquire a new customer. If you give away 1,000 branded water bottles at an event and can attribute 50 new customers directly from that promotion, your CPA is the total cost of those bottles divided by 50. This metric helps you determine whether your promotional products are actually driving new business.

Cost per Impression (CPI) measures how often your branding is seen per pound spent. A cheap, low-quality giveaway might get thrown away immediately, resulting in a high CPI. But a well-designed, high-value item—like a premium tote bag or insulated tumbler—will be used repeatedly, generating thousands of impressions over its lifetime and lowering your CPI.

The goal is to strike a balance. Some merchandise is meant to drive immediate conversions (low CPA), while others are designed for long-term brand visibility (low CPI). Understanding the difference helps you allocate budget effectively.

Measuring Engagement & Retention

Brand awareness is great, but engagement and retention are where the real money is. A well-executed merchandise strategy should do more than make people aware of your brand—it should keep them coming back.

To measure engagement, track how recipients interact with their merchandise. Are they sharing photos of it on social media? Are they wearing your branded apparel in public? You can monitor this by encouraging user-generated content with a specific hashtag, running contests that require people to post about their merch, or using QR codes that lead to a landing page where they can redeem an offer.

Retention is even more valuable. If your promotional products are part of a loyalty program or customer appreciation initiative, track how they impact repeat purchases. Do customers who receive merch spend more over time? Do they stay subscribed longer? Comparing retention rates between those who receive promotional items and those who don't will give you a clear picture of how well your strategy is working.

Another overlooked metric? Customer sentiment. Send a quick follow-up survey asking how recipients feel about the merchandise, whether they use it, and whether it influenced their perception of your brand. The insights will be invaluable.

A/B Testing Merchandise Effectiveness

If you're not testing, you're guessing. A/B testing—where you compare the effectiveness of two different strategies—is just as important for promotional merchandise as it is for ads, email marketing, or landing pages.

Start by testing different types of products. Let's say you're trying to decide between branded notebooks and stainless steel water bottles for a campaign. Give half your target audience notebooks and the other half water bottles, then track engagement, retention, and conversions for each group. Which item drives more social shares? Which results in more repeat purchases? The data will tell you what works best.

You can also test design variations. Maybe you're debating between a minimalistic logo placement versus a bold, eye-catching graphic. Send out both versions and see which gets more engagement.

Even distribution methods can be tested. Does giving away merch at live events generate better leads than sending it via direct mail? Does exclusive, members-only merch create more brand loyalty than mass giveaways? The only way to know for sure is to test.

The businesses that treat promotional merchandise like a science experiment—constantly testing, measuring, and refining—are the ones that turn branded merch into a serious revenue driver.

Digital Tracking Meets Physical Products

QR Codes and NFC Tech

Most promotional merchandise campaigns fail because they vanish into the abyss of forgotten freebies. You hand out a stack of branded tote bags, stress balls, or water bottles, and... nothing. No engagement, no data, no way to track if they made any impact. That's where smart tech—QR codes and NFC (Near Field Communication) tags—changes the game.

QR codes are simple, effective, and, thanks to smartphones, ridiculously easy for customers to use. Slap a QR code on your merch, and suddenly, that giveaway is a direct bridge to your website, a discount page, or an exclusive content hub. No more "hoping" people remember your brand—you're making it seamless for them to take action immediately.

But here's where most businesses get it wrong: they link the QR code to a generic homepage. That's a wasted opportunity. If you're giving away a branded notebook, the QR code should lead to something relevant—an exclusive ebook, a VIP discount, or a behind-the-scenes video about your brand. Make it feel like a secret door to something valuable, not just a link they could've Googled themselves.

NFC tech takes this a step further. Unlike QR codes, which require users to scan with their phone's camera, NFC tags trigger an action just by tapping a phone against them. Think of it like Apple Pay—just a quick tap, and they're in. You can embed NFC chips into high-end merchandise like custom keychains, coasters, or even clothing tags. One tap could take a customer to a personalised landing page, a special offer, or an interactive experience. It's effortless, which means more people will actually use it.

For events, this tech is priceless. Instead of handing out business cards that get lost or tossed, give out an NFC-enabled item that instantly saves your contact info when tapped. Now you're memorable, and more importantly, you're in their phone—right where you want to be.

Landing Pages & Unique Discount Codes

A common mistake with promotional merchandise is assuming that just having your logo on something is enough. It's not. You need a way to measure whether that merch is actually driving engagement and sales. That's where dedicated landing pages and unique discount codes come in.

A dedicated landing page gives you control over the customer's experience. Instead of sending them to your homepage (where they'll likely get distracted and leave), direct them to a page designed specifically for that piece of merch. If you're handing out branded coffee mugs at a trade show, the landing page could feature a special offer on your products, a giveaway entry form, or a short video about your company. Make sure the page is laser-focused—one clear call to action, no fluff.

Unique discount codes are another powerful tool. Instead of giving out a generic "10% OFF" code that could be shared online by anyone, create merch-specific codes. If you're distributing branded tote bags at an event, print a code like "TOTE10" inside them. Now, when someone redeems that code online, you know exactly where they came from. This lets you track which promotional items are actually working and which ones are just getting tossed in a drawer.

Want to take it a step further? Use personalised QR codes or NFC chips that generate unique discount links for each user. Now you're not just tracking general engagement—you're tracking individual customer journeys. That's next-level data.

Social Media Engagement Tracking

Promotional merchandise isn't just about physical products— it's about starting conversations. If you're not using merch to drive social media engagement, you're leaving serious brand awareness on the table.

The easiest way to do this? Turn your merch into a social media challenge. Include a call-to-action on your products— something like "Snap a pic with this and tag us @yourbrand for a surprise!" This leverages user-generated content (UGC), which is far more effective than anything you could create yourself. People trust other people more than they trust brands, so when they see real customers sharing your merch, it builds credibility and buzz.

Hashtags are another simple but powerful tool. Create a unique hashtag for your merch campaign and print it directly on the product packaging. If you're running a giveaway, make the hashtag part of the entry process—"Post a pic with #MyBrand-

Merch for a chance to win!" This not only boosts engagement but also gives you an easy way to track how many people are actually using your merch in the wild.

If you want to go deeper, integrate your merch campaign with social media analytics tools. Platforms like Instagram and Twitter allow you to monitor hashtag performance, mentions, and engagement rates. If you notice that certain products generate more posts and shares than others, you've just identified the winners in your merch lineup. Double down on what's working and ditch what's not.

For high-ticket giveaways, consider using social media contests where users have to tag friends, follow your page, or share a post to enter. This turns one piece of merch into exponential brand exposure. Instead of just one person seeing your brand, their entire network does. That's free marketing at scale.

Promotional merchandise works best when it's not just a give-away but a conversation starter. By integrating digital tracking tools—QR codes, NFC tech, landing pages, unique discount codes, and social media—you're not just throwing products into the void. You're creating a measurable, data-driven system that turns every piece of merch into an active marketing asset.

Analysing and Adapting for Better Results

Identifying Underperforming Products

If your promotional merch isn't pulling its weight, it's dead weight. Every pound spent on ineffective giveaways is money that could've been better spent elsewhere. The problem? Most businesses don't take the time to analyse what's working and what isn't. They assume that because they've given something away, it's automatically valuable. It's not.

Start by looking at the basics:

- **Are people actually using it?** If your branded tote bags are sitting in the back of a cupboard instead of being carried around, they're not increasing brand visibility. If your custom pens disappear into desk drawers never to be seen again, they're not doing their job either.
- **Is it generating engagement?** Track how many people redeem the QR code you've printed on your merch. Monitor website visits from custom URLs tied to your giveaways. If no one is scanning, clicking, or engaging, the product is failing.
- **Are customers talking about it?** Great merch creates conversation. If people aren't sharing it on social media, mentioning it in reviews, or using it in public, it's probably forgettable.

To pinpoint underperformance, compare different products over time. A well-designed keyring might outperform an expensive hoodie if it's something people actually use daily. A tech gadget may seem exciting but could be too complicated or irrelevant to your audience. The key is to identify patterns and adjust accordingly.

If a product isn't working, don't cling to it just because you've already invested in inventory. Cut your losses and reallocate that budget into something that delivers better results.

Scaling What Works

Once you've identified the top performers, the next step is to maximise their impact. Doubling down on what works is how you move from mediocre results to real, measurable gains.

A winning product isn't just something people like – it's something they actively use and associate with your brand. If a particular item is gaining traction, scale it up intelligently:

- **Increase distribution** – If a certain piece of merch is driving engagement, get it into more hands. Expand its availability at trade shows, add it to online orders, or use it in direct mail campaigns.
- **Enhance the experience** – Take a popular item and refine it. If your audience loves your branded notebooks, consider upgrading to a premium version with better materials. If a particular hoodie is a hit, offer it in different colours or limited-edition designs.
- **Tie it to a campaign** – Use successful merch as part of a larger marketing strategy. If a specific product has high engagement, integrate it with your referral programme, loyalty incentives, or social media contests.

Scaling doesn't mean blindly producing more of the same. It

means refining, optimising, and leveraging what's already working to create even better results. The goal is to turn a good idea into a powerhouse marketing tool.

When to Retire a Merchandise Campaign

Not all merch is meant to last forever. Trends shift, customer preferences evolve, and what worked last year might not be relevant today. The best brands know when to pull the plug on a product before it becomes stale.

Consider these signs that it's time to retire a merchandise campaign:

· **Declining engagement** – If fewer people are redeeming discount codes, scanning QR links, or posting about your merch, interest is waning.
· **Market saturation** – If you've been handing out the same item for years, chances are your audience has already received it (maybe more than once). Time to switch things up.
· **Brand evolution** – If your company has rebranded, updated its messaging, or shifted focus, your promo products should reflect that change. Outdated branding on old merch weakens your overall image.
· **Cost vs. value** – If the price of producing a specific item has increased but the ROI hasn't, it might not be worth continuing. Find something more cost-effective that delivers better impact.

Retiring a product doesn't mean you've wasted money—it means you're staying ahead of the curve. Smart businesses constantly refine their strategies, ensuring their promotional merchandise remains fresh, relevant, and effective.

9

THINK LIKE A BIG BRAND – HOW INDUSTRY LEADERS MASTER PROMOTIONAL MERCHANDISE

"A brand is no longer what we tell the consumer it is—it is what consumers tell each other it is." — *Scott Cook*

WHAT BIG BRANDS DO DIFFERENTLY

Consistency Across All Touchpoints

The most powerful brands don't just slap their logo on a T-shirt and call it a day. They weave their identity into everything they touch—every product, every ad, every interaction. This is the difference between a forgettable giveaway and a piece of merch that becomes an extension of your brand.

Think about Apple. Whether you're holding an iPhone, unboxing AirPods, or walking into one of their stores, the experience is seamless. Everything is designed to reinforce the brand's identity—clean, minimalist, premium. Their merch, from employee T-shirts to WWDC swag, follows the same formula.

When you create promotional merchandise, it needs to feel like a natural part of your brand, not an afterthought. If your company is known for high-end services, giving away cheap plastic keychains sends the wrong message. If sustainability is central to your identity, your merch should reflect that—think organic cotton tote bags, recycled notebooks, or reusable water bottles.

Your audience expects consistency. The moment your merch feels disconnected from your brand, you lose credibility. Every item you put out into the world should reinforce your message, your aesthetic, and your values.

Long-Term Merch Strategies

Most companies treat promotional merchandise like a one-off marketing expense. Big brands don't. They treat it as an investment in long-term brand equity.

Nike doesn't just sell sportswear; it sells a lifestyle. Owning Nike gear means being part of an elite club of athletes and achievers. Their promotional merchandise follows the same playbook—limited drops, collaborations, and high-quality materials that people actually want to wear.

Your merch strategy should go beyond trade shows and swag bags. Think about how you can create a long-term system where your merchandise continues to build brand awareness and customer loyalty:

- **Seasonal drops:** Instead of random giveaways, release exclusive merch tied to seasons, holidays, or major company milestones.
- **Loyalty rewards:** Offer premium merchandise as a reward for repeat customers or top clients. A well-designed, high-end hoodie given to your best customers does more for brand retention than a generic pen handed out to everyone.
- **Employee culture:** Some of your best brand ambassadors are your employees. High-quality internal merch—branded jackets, premium notebooks, stylish drinkware—turns your team into walking billboards for your brand.

Merchandise should be a tool for deepening engagement, not just an item that gets handed out and forgotten. Big brands understand this, and they approach their promotional products the same way they approach any other part of their marketing strategy—with a long-term vision.

High-Quality Over Cheap Giveaways

The fastest way to waste money on promotional merchandise is to go cheap. The fastest way to build brand equity with merchandise is to go premium.

Think of the last time you received a flimsy, logo-heavy T-shirt from a company. Did you wear it? Probably not. Now think of those high-quality branded water bottles, sleek notebooks, or minimalist tote bags that people actually use daily. These products don't just get noticed; they create lasting impressions.

Big brands understand that quality equals perception. This is why companies like Tesla sell premium branded apparel and accessories that feel like an extension of their products. Their hats, jackets, and backpacks aren't just another piece of merch; they're designed with the same sleek, futuristic aesthetic as their cars.

If you're choosing between ordering 5,000 cheap plastic pens or 500 premium metal ones, go with the latter. A high-quality product will last longer, get used more often, and create a stronger association with your brand.

Here's how to ensure your merch meets the high standards of top brands:

- **Materials matter:** Opt for durable, well-crafted items. If it feels cheap, it reflects poorly on your brand.
- **Design with intention:** Subtle branding, premium packaging, and an aesthetic that aligns with your company make all the difference.
- **Functionality first:** The best promotional items are things people actually use—reusable water bottles, stylish tote bags, sleek notebooks, or even high-end tech gadgets.

Every piece of merch you create is a representation of your brand. If it feels premium, your brand feels premium. If it's cheap and disposable, so is the impression it leaves behind.

Creating a Cult-Like Following Through Merch

The Power of Brand Loyalty

A strong brand doesn't just have customers—it has fans. The kind of people who proudly wear your logo, talk about your products without being asked, and feel a personal connection to your company. This level of loyalty doesn't happen by accident. It's built through consistent engagement, emotional resonance, and, yes, the right promotional merchandise.

When people feel like they're part of something bigger than just a transaction, they stick around. They don't just buy from you; they advocate for you. Whether it's a recognisable coffee chain with reusable cups that double as a status symbol or a streetwear brand whose limited-run T-shirts sell out in minutes, the connection goes beyond the product itself.

Merchandise plays a huge role in fostering this kind of loyalty. Wearing a brand is a statement—it signals belonging, shared values, and personal identity. When people proudly wear or use your merch, they're reinforcing their connection to your brand every single day.

The key is to create merchandise that doesn't feel like a cheap giveaway. It should feel like an exclusive membership badge, something people are proud to own. The moment you shift from "free stuff" to "must-have gear," you've moved from customer engagement to full-blown brand loyalty.

Look at how brands like Harley-Davidson operate. Their

customers aren't just buying motorcycles—they're buying a lifestyle. The brand's clothing and accessories aren't just extras; they're essential parts of the experience. You don't see Harley fans wearing knock-off gear—they want the real thing because it represents who they are. That's the level of emotional investment you should aim for with your promotional merchandise.

How Exclusivity Creates Demand

Scarcity drives desire. When something isn't available to everyone, it becomes more valuable. This is why limited-edition merch sells out fast and why people queue for hours to get their hands on exclusive drops.

The psychology behind this is simple: when people believe they might miss out, they act fast. They don't hesitate, they don't overthink—they buy. And once they have that exclusive item, they feel a sense of belonging to a select group. This is why luxury brands can charge premium prices for basic items with a logo on them. The value isn't just in the product—it's in the exclusivity.

You can use this same principle for your brand, no matter your industry. Limited-edition merchandise, collaborations with influencers, or VIP-only product drops—all of these create urgency and excitement. People don't just want your merch; they need it before it's gone.

Think about how major brands handle their product launches. Nike's trainer drops sell out in minutes because they create anticipation and scarcity. They don't just put their new designs on shelves and hope people buy them. They build hype, create waiting lists, and release only a small batch at a time. The result? Demand skyrockets.

Your merchandise can work the same way. Instead of handing out free T-shirts to anyone who walks by at an event, create a limited run of premium-quality shirts available only to your top customers or most engaged community members. Instead of ordering thousands of generic pens, release an exclusive, beautifully designed notebook that only a small group of people can get their hands on.

When the supply is limited, the value increases. People start talking. They want to be part of the inner circle. And once they have your merch, they're not just using it—they're showing it off.

Limited Drops & Pre-Sales

One of the most powerful ways to build demand is by using limited drops and pre-sales. This creates anticipation and ensures that people act fast instead of waiting around to decide if they want your merch.

A limited drop means you're only releasing a certain number of items, and once they're gone, they're gone. This taps into the fear of missing out (FOMO) and makes people more likely to buy immediately. It also generates buzz—people start talking, sharing, and showing off their exclusive merch.

Pre-sales take this a step further. When you allow people to order before the official release, you not only guarantee sales but also build excitement. Think about how Apple launches its products. They announce a new iPhone, open up pre-orders, and watch as millions of people rush to secure their spot. The result? Long waiting lists and a brand that feels highly coveted.

You can do this with your promotional merchandise. Instead of ordering thousands of items upfront and hoping they get used, launch a pre-sale campaign. Let your audience know that only a limited number of items will be available and that they need to act fast if they want one.

This approach works especially well when combined with exclusivity. Maybe your limited merch drop is only available to your most loyal customers. Maybe it's part of a collaboration with an industry influencer. Maybe it's a special-edition item that won't be made again. The key is to make people feel like they're getting in on something special.

Streetwear brands have mastered this strategy. Brands like Supreme release small batches of products that sell out instantly. They don't overproduce. They don't try to make their merch available to everyone. Instead, they limit supply, creating a sense of urgency and exclusivity.

Your business can do the same thing. Even if you're in B2B, you can use limited drops to engage your audience. Instead of sending generic swag to every client, create a premium, exclusive item that only your top-tier customers receive. If you're running an event, offer VIP attendees access to a special edition piece of merch that won't be available to the general public.

The moment people realise they can't just grab your merch whenever they want, they'll want it even more. And when they do get it, they'll value it—not just for what it is, but for what it represents.

Applying Big Brand Tactics to Small Businesses

Leveraging Partnerships

You don't need the budget of a global brand to create high-impact promotional merchandise. One of the smartest ways to maximise your reach without draining resources is by leveraging strategic partnerships. Big brands do this all the time—think Nike collaborating with Apple on fitness tech, or luxury fashion houses teaming up with streetwear labels to create high-demand limited drops. You can apply the same principles to your business, regardless of size.

Start by identifying complementary businesses that share your audience but aren't direct competitors. If you're a local coffee brand, partner with a popular bakery to create co-branded mugs or reusable cups. If you run a fitness studio, collaborate with an activewear brand on custom workout gear. When two brands align on a piece of merchandise, you both gain exposure to each other's audiences with a fraction of the usual marketing spend.

The key is to ensure that both brands add value to the product. A cheap pen with two logos slapped on it won't move the needle. Instead, create something that genuinely enhances the customer experience—something they'll actually want to use daily. A high-quality tote bag featuring artwork from a local designer, co-branded between a bookstore and a publishing house, lives in a customer's life far longer than a generic freebie.

You can also tap into influencer partnerships. Many emerging brands make the mistake of thinking influencer collaborations are only for big corporations with deep pockets. The reality is that micro-influencers (those with 10,000–100,000 highly engaged followers) can be even more effective than celebrities. Instead of paying a hefty fee for a one-time post, send influencers exclusive, well-designed merch that aligns with their lifestyle. If they genuinely love it, they'll wear it, use it, and share it with their audience. That organic endorsement is more powerful than any paid ad.

Getting More with Less Budget

Big brands have an advantage when it comes to budget, but that doesn't mean you need deep pockets to compete. The trick is making every pound—or dollar—count by focusing on quality over quantity. A well-made, carefully chosen piece of merchandise will have a far greater impact than handing out thousands of forgettable, low-quality items.

One way to stretch your budget is by being selective about who gets your merch. Instead of giving away branded products to anyone who walks by your booth at a trade show, reserve them for people who engage with your business in a meaningful way— high-value prospects, loyal customers, or those who participate in a specific activation. This not only reduces waste but also increases the perceived value of your merchandise.

Another tactic is bulk ordering strategically. Many suppliers offer significant price breaks at certain quantities, but that doesn't mean you need to order thousands of units to get a good deal. Work with manufacturers who offer "split production," allowing you to order multiple designs or product variations under one bulk pricing tier. This lets you test different styles without committing to a single design in massive quantities.

Consider pre-selling your merchandise rather than giving it all away for free. Limited-edition branded products can be positioned as exclusive items customers can purchase rather than just receive. If your audience sees others paying for your merch, it instantly elevates its perceived value. A well-executed pre-sale campaign can even fund the production costs before you've spent a penny.

Building a Merchandise Ecosystem

The best brands don't just distribute promotional merchandise; they create a full ecosystem around it. Instead of treating merch as a one-off marketing expense, you can integrate it into your business model as an ongoing revenue stream or engagement tool.

One way to do this is by turning your merch into a reward system. Customers who spend over a certain amount, refer a friend, or hit a milestone can receive exclusive branded products. This approach transforms merch from a passive giveaway into an active driver of customer behaviour.

Subscription-based merchandise is another strategy that big brands use, and it's something you can adapt to your business. Think of how beauty brands offer subscription boxes featuring curated products or how coffee brands sell monthly memberships that include exclusive branded items. If you run an e-commerce store, a quarterly merch drop tied to special promotions or loyalty rewards keeps customers engaged and excited.

A merchandise ecosystem also includes strategic product bundling. Instead of just giving away standalone branded items, integrate them into a larger purchase. A clothing brand can include a limited-edition tote bag with every order over £100. A SaaS company can send exclusive branded notebooks to customers who sign up for an annual plan instead of a monthly subscription.

By weaving merchandise into the fabric of your business strategy, you're no longer just handing out free stuff—you're creating a system where your merch actively contributes to customer retention, brand loyalty, and long-term profitability.

10

SUSTAINABILITY & ETHICAL CONSIDERATIONS – WINNING WITHOUT WASTING

"The greatest threat to our planet is the belief that someone else will save it."
– Robert Swan

THE SHIFT TOWARDS ECO-FRIENDLY MERCHANDISE

Why Customers Care About Sustainability

Sustainability is no longer a "nice to have" – it's an expectation. Customers are demanding more from the brands they support, and that includes the merchandise they receive. A cheap plastic giveaway that ends up in the bin within hours does more harm than good. It signals wastefulness, lack of foresight, and a disconnect from modern consumer values. You don't want your brand associated with landfill.

Your customers are more informed than ever. They're scruti-nising supply chains, calling out greenwashing, and choosing brands that align with their values. Studies show that 73% of global consumers are willing to change their consumption habits to reduce environmental impact. That's not just a passing trend – it's a shift in behaviour that directly affects purchasing decisions.

When your promotional merchandise aligns with these values, it strengthens trust and loyalty. People feel good about supporting a brand that makes responsible choices. And when they use sustainable merch in their daily lives – a high-quality tote bag, a reusable coffee cup, or a biodegradable notebook – they're not just using a product. They're carrying a statement, a reflection of their values, and an extension of your brand's commitment to something bigger than profit.

Choosing Ethical Suppliers

Sustainable merchandise starts long before it reaches your customer's hands. It begins with the suppliers you choose. If you're serious about eco-friendly merch, dig deeper than the buzzwords. "Made from recycled materials" or "eco-conscious" means nothing without proof. Transparency is key.

Look for suppliers that provide certifications like FSC (Forest Stewardship Council), GOTS (Global Organic Textile Standard), Fair Trade, or B Corp certification. These labels indicate re-sponsible sourcing, ethical labour practices, and environmental responsibility. If your supplier can't tell you where their materials come from or how their workers are treated, that's a red flag.

Avoid companies that claim sustainability but can't back it up with data. Ask specific questions:

- Where are your materials sourced?
- What is your carbon footprint?
- How are workers compensated?
- Do you have certifications to verify your claims?

And don't just take their word for it. Visit factories if possible, or request third-party audits. Ethical sourcing isn't just about sustainability – it's about integrity. When you align your business with suppliers who genuinely care, your merchandise carries the weight of authenticity. Customers can feel the difference.

Reducing Plastic Waste

Plastic is the enemy of sustainability. It lingers for centuries, pollutes oceans, and contributes to the growing environmental crisis. The last thing you want is for your brand to be responsible for more plastic waste. The good news? There are alternatives that don't compromise on quality or impact.

Start by eliminating single-use plastics. If you're still handing out plastic water bottles, disposable pens, or cheap keychains, it's time for a rethink. Instead, opt for:

- **Bamboo or stainless steel reusable bottles** – A gift people actually use daily.
- **Recycled paper or seed-paper notebooks** – Functional, responsible, and biodegradable.
- **Organic cotton tote bags** – A stylish and durable alternative to plastic bags.
- **Plant-based or biodegradable phone cases** – Tech accessories with a lower footprint.

Another overlooked factor? Packaging. Many brands focus on sustainable products but overlook the excessive plastic wrapping they come in. Choose compostable mailers, recycled cardboard boxes, and soy-based inks for printing. The goal is to create an end-to-end sustainable experience.

If you're worried about costs, remember: sustainability isn't just an expense – it's an investment. It strengthens your brand reputation, builds deeper customer loyalty, and even opens doors to eco-conscious partnerships. Consumers are willing to pay more for sustainable products because they see the value. When you position your brand as part of the solution, you differentiate yourself from competitors who are still stuck in outdated merchandising tactics.

Sustainable merchandise isn't about jumping on a trend. It's about future-proofing your brand.

Avoiding "Throwaway" Promotional Products

Investing in Quality Over Quantity

There's a reason why the best brands don't cheap out on their promotional merchandise. You've seen it before—companies handing out flimsy plastic keychains or pens that barely write. These items don't just get ignored; they actively damage your brand. If your merch feels disposable, so does your company.

Instead of flooding people with low-cost, low-value items, focus on quality. A well-made product that lasts is a walking, talking billboard for your brand. Think about a premium insulated water bottle versus a thin plastic cup. One gets used daily, the other ends up in the bin within hours.

The trick is to choose merchandise that people actually want to keep. Higher-quality items might have a slightly higher price tag, but they also have a far greater lifespan and impact. A durable tote bag, a sleek notebook with premium paper, or a stylish cap with subtle branding—these are the things people hang onto.

The goal isn't just to put your logo on something. It's to create an item that integrates into your customer's life. If your product is useful and well made, it won't just be another freebie—it will be part of their daily routine. And that's where the real brand awareness happens.

Reusable & Functional Items

If you want your merch to stick around, it needs to serve a purpose. The best promotional products aren't just branded; they're functional. And if they're reusable, even better.

A reusable item means repeat exposure. Think about a high-quality coffee cup—every morning, your customer grabs it, takes it to work, and your brand gets seen. Compare that to a single-use plastic cup with your logo. One lasts years, the other lasts minutes.

Functionality also plays a huge role. If a product doesn't serve a practical purpose, it won't get used. Simple rule: If you wouldn't use it yourself, don't expect others to.

Some of the best reusable and functional promotional products include:

- **Tech accessories** – Wireless chargers, cable organisers, USB hubs.
- **Office essentials** – Premium notebooks, sleek pens, desktop organisers.
- **Everyday carry items** – Keyring multitools, reusable shopping bags, insulated flasks.
- **Health & wellness products** – Resistance bands, yoga mats, stainless steel water bottles.

The best merch isn't just something people use—it's something they love using. When an item fits seamlessly into someone's life, they don't just keep it; they rely on it. And when they rely on it, they form a stronger connection with your brand.

Smart Packaging Solutions

The first impression of your promotional merchandise isn't the product—it's the packaging. If you're handing out high-quality merch but wrapping it in cheap, wasteful plastic, you're sending mixed signals. Your packaging should align with your brand values and enhance the overall experience.

Minimalism is key. Excess packaging doesn't just cost more—it creates unnecessary waste. The best solution is to keep it simple and sustainable. Think recycled kraft paper, reusable pouches, or even stylish cardboard boxes that can be repurposed.

Brands that get this right make the unboxing experience part of the appeal. A sleek, well-designed box or pouch adds perceived value before the recipient even sees what's inside. If it feels premium, it is premium.

Some smart packaging ideas:

- **Seed paper wrapping** – Instead of tossing it, recipients can plant it and grow wildflowers.
- **Reusable fabric pouches** – A great alternative to plastic and adds a touch of luxury.
- **Foldable kraft boxes** – Sturdy enough to keep and reuse, reducing waste.
- **Minimalist recycled paper wraps** – Simple, elegant, and eco-friendly.

Your packaging should be as intentional as your product choice. If your brand is about quality and sustainability, your packaging needs to reflect that. A well-packaged item feels special, and when something feels special, it doesn't get thrown away.

Positioning Your Brand as Socially Responsible

Marketing Your Sustainability Efforts

Sustainability isn't just a buzzword; it's a competitive advantage. Customers are paying attention, and they expect brands to do more than just talk about being eco-friendly—they want to see action. If you're investing in sustainable merchandise, you need to communicate it effectively. The brands that win in this space don't bury their sustainability efforts in a footnote on their website; they make it a core part of their identity.

Start with your packaging and product labelling. If your promotional merch is made from recycled materials, say so—clearly. If it supports a social cause, make it obvious. A simple tag that reads, "Made from 100% recycled materials" or "Every purchase helps plant a tree" immediately signals to the customer that this is more than just another freebie.

Your marketing should highlight the why behind your sustainable choices. Did you switch to organic cotton because it reduces water consumption by 91% compared to conventional cotton? Say that. Did you eliminate plastic from your packaging because 91% of plastic waste never gets recycled? Make that point. People respond to stories, not vague claims. Show them how your brand is making a difference, and they'll be more likely to align with you.

Leverage social proof. If customers love your eco-friendly merch, let them share their experiences. Encourage user-generated content by asking people to post about your sustainable products on social media. Feature testimonials from clients who appreciate your commitment to ethical business practices. When other people advocate for your sustainability efforts, it carries far more weight than any marketing copy you write yourself.

Transparency is key. If you're making sustainable claims, back them up with facts. If your T-shirts are made from organic cotton, specify the certification (e.g., GOTS-certified). If your tote bags are made from recycled plastic bottles, state how many bottles were repurposed. Specificity builds trust, and trust builds loyal customers.

Make your sustainability efforts easy to share. Provide pre-written social media captions or hashtags that customers can use when they receive your merch. A well-placed QR code linking to a short video about your sustainability mission can turn a simple giveaway into a brand-building moment.

Sustainability isn't just a side note—it's a selling point. If you're doing the work to make your promotional merchandise eco-friendly, shout about it from the rooftops.

Aligning with Ethical Causes

Customers don't just buy products; they buy into brands that align with their values. When your promotional merchandise supports an ethical cause, it becomes more than just a marketing tool—it becomes a symbol of shared beliefs.

The key is authenticity. If your brand has never spoken about environmental issues and suddenly starts giving away bamboo straws, it's going to feel like a gimmick. But if sustainability is woven into your business model—whether through ethical sourcing, carbon offsetting, or charitable partnerships—your promotional merchandise can reinforce that commitment.

One of the most effective ways to align with ethical causes is through direct collaboration. Partner with non-profits, charities, or social enterprises that align with your brand values. If you're in the fitness industry, work with an organisation that promotes clean water access. If you're in tech, support an initiative that recycles e-waste. The partnership should feel natural, not forced.

Don't just donate a percentage of profits—make it tangible. If you're giving away sustainable promotional merchandise, tie it to real action. "For every reusable water bottle we distribute, we remove 1kg of plastic from the ocean." That's a statement people can get behind. It turns a simple piece of merch into a movement.

Events are another great way to align with ethical causes. Instead of just handing out swag at a trade show, set up an

109

interactive booth where attendees can learn about the impact of their choices. Host a sustainability challenge where participants pledge to reduce their plastic use in exchange for an eco-friendly giveaway. Make it engaging, and they'll remember your brand long after the event ends.

The best partnerships are mutually beneficial. The organisation you support gets increased visibility and funding, while your brand earns trust and goodwill from socially conscious consumers. It's a win-win.

But here's the key—consistency matters. If you support an ethical cause today and forget about it next quarter, it looks performative. If you want to position your brand as socially responsible, it has to be a long-term strategy, not a one-off marketing stunt.

Turning CSR Into a Competitive Advantage

Corporate social responsibility (CSR) isn't just about doing good—it's about standing out in a crowded market. Customers are increasingly choosing brands based on their ethical practices, and companies that integrate CSR into their promotional merchandise strategy gain a serious competitive edge.

Think of CSR-driven merch as a way to differentiate yourself. If your competitors are handing out cheap plastic keychains while you're giving away biodegradable phone cases, who do you think leaves a stronger impression? The more thoughtful and aligned your merchandise is with your CSR initiatives, the more powerful it becomes as a brand-building tool.

One of the most effective ways to integrate CSR into your merchandise strategy is by making your customers part of the impact. Instead of just telling them your brand is socially responsible, let them experience it firsthand. Offer a choice: "Would you like a free eco-friendly notebook, or would you prefer we plant a tree in your name?" Not only does this engage the customer, but it also reinforces your commitment to sustainability in a memorable way.

Limited-edition CSR merchandise can create exclusivity while promoting a cause. If you release a special line of promotional products where a portion of proceeds supports an environmental initiative, it adds perceived value. Customers aren't just receiving a giveaway; they're participating in something bigger than themselves.

Internal adoption of CSR-focused merchandise is just as important as external marketing. Equip your employees with sustainable branded products—reusable coffee cups, organic cotton uniforms, or recycled-material laptop sleeves. If your team embodies your sustainability values, it strengthens your brand's credibility. When employees believe in the mission, they become natural advocates who spread the message organically.

CSR-driven merchandise can also enhance customer retention. A brand that consistently reinforces its values through high-quality, ethically sourced merchandise builds deeper relationships with its audience. When customers feel good about supporting a brand, they stick around.

The final advantage? Positive PR. When your CSR initiatives are genuinely impactful, they become newsworthy. Media coverage, industry recognition, and word-of-mouth buzz all contribute to brand authority. Sustainable merchandise isn't just about making an impression on the recipient—it's about amplifying your impact far beyond the initial interaction.

CSR isn't a marketing gimmick; it's a long-term strategy that positions your brand as one that truly cares. And when done right, it's not just good for the planet—it's good for business.

11

CRAFTING YOUR ULTIMATE PROMOTIONAL MERCH STRATEGY

"Give me six hours to chop down a tree and I will spend the first four sharpening the axe." – Abraham Lincoln

Building Your Customised Merch Plan

Promotional merchandise can be a powerful tool—when it's done right. But too many businesses treat it as an afterthought, throwing money at random products in the hope they'll magically boost brand awareness or drive sales. That's a recipe for wasted budgets and underwhelming results.

If you want merch that actually works, you need a plan. A clear, structured approach that aligns with your objectives, brand identity, and—most importantly—what your customers actually want. This isn't about slapping your logo on cheap giveaways. It's about creating something that people value, use, and associate with your brand in a meaningful way.

Let's break it down.

Defining Your Goals and Budget

Before you even think about what merch to create, you need to answer one simple question: What do you want it to achieve?

Are you looking to generate leads? Strengthen brand loyalty? Increase sales? Drive social media engagement? Each goal requires a different strategy—and different products.

For example, if you're trying to capture leads at an event, your merch should be something enticing enough that people willingly hand over their contact details. If you're aiming to boost word-of-mouth, you might focus on high-quality clothing that turns customers into walking ambassadors.

Once your objective is clear, set a budget that makes sense. This isn't about spending the least amount possible—it's about maximising impact. A £1 plastic pen that gets thrown away is a waste of money. A £10 premium notebook that gets used for months? That's brand exposure on repeat.

Break your budget down into three key areas:

1. **Production Costs** – The actual cost of the items, including materials and printing.
2. **Distribution Costs** – Shipping, packaging, and logistics.
3. **Marketing & Integration** – How the merch fits into your campaigns, whether that's event giveaways, influencer collaborations, or direct mail strategies.

Plan your budget with long-term impact in mind. A smaller batch of high-quality products will always be more effective than mass-distributing cheap, forgettable junk.

Choosing the Right Products

Now that you've nailed down your goals and budget, it's time to select the right merchandise. The biggest mistake you can make here is choosing something just because it's cheap or popular. The best promotional products are those that fit seamlessly into your customers' daily lives.

Three key factors to consider:

1. **Utility** – Will people actually use this? A branded tote bag, high-quality water bottle, or stylish hoodie is far more effective than a gimmicky stress ball that ends up in the bin.
2. **Brand Alignment** – Your merch should reflect your brand's personality and values. A luxury watch brand shouldn't be handing out flimsy plastic keyrings. A sustainable company shouldn't be giving away single-use plastic items.
3. **Perceived Value** – The higher the perceived value, the more likely people are to keep and appreciate the item. A sleek, well-designed product will always outperform something that looks cheap or generic.

Think about how your merch can integrate into your customers' daily routines. A beautifully designed notebook? Used every day. A well-made hoodie? Worn regularly. A high-quality phone stand? Sat on their desk for months. These aren't just promotional items—they're constant brand reminders.

Another pro move? Limited edition or exclusive items. If people feel like they're getting something special, they'll value it more. Create a sense of scarcity—whether it's a limited run of custom T-shirts or an exclusive design only available at a particular event. People love getting their hands on something unique.

Mapping Out Distribution Channels

Even the best merchandise is useless if it never reaches the right people. Distribution is just as important as the product itself.

Start by asking: Where does it make the most sense to get this into customers' hands?

Some of the most effective channels include:

- **Events & Trade Shows** – High-quality, well-designed giveaways can drive foot traffic and spark conversations. But don't just hand them out to anyone—make sure there's an exchange of value, like gathering contact details or scheduling follow-ups.
- **Direct Mail Campaigns** – A carefully curated merch package can cut through the digital noise and create a tangible connection with your audience. Pair it with a handwritten note and watch engagement soar.
- **Online Orders & Upsells** – Including a free piece of merch with a purchase can enhance customer experience and increase brand loyalty. A surprise extra in a package can

turn a one-time buyer into a repeat customer.

· **Influencer & Ambassador Partnerships** – Co-branded merchandise with influencers or industry leaders can massively extend your brand reach. The key is choosing partners who genuinely align with your brand.
· **Employee Advocacy Programmes** – Your team should be your biggest brand ambassadors. High-quality branded apparel or accessories can turn employees into walking billboards—and they'll proudly wear them if they actually look good.

Distribution isn't just about handing things out—it's about making sure they end up in the right hands. A limited number of highly targeted giveaways will always outperform mass distribution to the wrong audience.

And don't forget about the packaging and presentation. A premium product deserves premium packaging. Even something as simple as good design, eco-friendly materials, or a personalised note can elevate the perceived value of your merch.

Promotional merchandise isn't just about giving things away—it's about creating a lasting impact. A well-thought-out strategy ensures that every item you produce serves a purpose, aligns with your brand, and delivers real value to your audience.

Avoiding Common Mistakes in Execution

Poor Timing & Seasonal Oversights

Timing is everything. You can have the most innovative, high-quality promotional merch in the world, but if it arrives too late or is irrelevant to the moment, it's a wasted opportunity.

A classic mistake? Ordering summer-themed merch in September or giving out heavy winter scarves in April. Seasonal relevance matters. If your merch doesn't fit the time of year, it won't get used, and if it doesn't get used, it won't drive engagement or brand awareness.

Event timing is just as crucial. You don't want your promo items arriving the day after a major trade show or landing in customers' hands after they've already made their buying decisions. Get ahead of the game by planning production and shipping timelines with a buffer. Suppliers can have delays, customs can be unpredictable, and last-minute rush orders will cost you more and compromise quality.

For product launches, sync your merch with the hype cycle. If you're launching a new product or service, your promo items should build anticipation before the launch, reinforce the message during, and keep the momentum going after. A three-phase approach ensures your merch isn't just a one-off giveaway but a strategic tool in your marketing arsenal.

Then there's the issue of giving away the wrong thing at the wrong time. A heavy-duty power bank is a great promo item—except when you're handing it out at a fitness expo where attendees are carrying minimal gear. A high-end notebook is fantastic—until you give it away at a digital marketing conference where everyone takes notes on their laptop. Context matters as much as the product itself.

Overcomplicating the Design Process

A beautifully designed piece of merchandise can be a walking advertisement for your brand. But too many businesses complicate the design process, leading to merch that's either cluttered, illegible, or just plain off-brand.

The first mistake is trying to do too much. Your logo, tagline, website, social media handle, mission statement, and a QR code all crammed onto a single tote bag? That's not branding—it's noise. Keep it simple. A clean design with strong branding is far more effective than a cluttered mess that gets ignored.

Branding should be recognisable but not overpowering. Subtle branding often works better than a giant logo slapped across the front of a product. Think about how brands like Nike and Apple handle their merch—they don't need to spell out their name in bold letters, and neither do you. A well-placed, minimal logo can make an item feel premium rather than promotional.

Another common misstep is not considering the actual use case. A T-shirt design might look great on a screen but be unreadable when worn. A mug with a detailed design might look fantastic in a mock-up but lose all its detail when printed on a curved surface. Work with designers who understand merchandise printing and production constraints.

119

Don't forget about colour psychology. The colours you choose should align with your brand and evoke the right emotions. Bright, energetic colours can work well in industries like fitness or entertainment, while muted, sophisticated tones might be better for luxury brands or corporate settings.

Finally, test before mass production. Always get a physical sample before committing to a large order. What looks good on a digital proof might not translate well in real life. The texture, print quality, and colour accuracy need to be checked before you invest in thousands of units.

Ignoring Customer Feedback

One of the biggest mistakes in promotional merchandise? Assuming you know what people want without actually asking them.

You might think a branded keychain is a great idea—until you realise no one actually uses keychains anymore. You might believe a tote bag is a safe bet—until you find out your audience already has a dozen of them and doesn't need another. The best way to know what will resonate? Ask your customers.

Use surveys, social media polls, and direct feedback to understand what types of merchandise your audience actually values. Look at past campaigns—what got used, what got ignored, what generated buzz? Data from previous promotions can help you refine future choices.

Another overlooked tactic: watch how people interact with your merch in real time. If you're at an event, pay attention to what attendees do with the giveaways. Do they immediately stash it in their bag and forget about it? Do they start using it right away? Do they trade it for something else? The way people engage with your merch tells you everything you need to know about its effectiveness.

Post-campaign, track engagement metrics. If you include a QR code or a discount code with your merch, monitor how many people actually use it. If you send out branded notebooks, see if customers post about them on social media. If no one is engaging, that's a sign you might need to rethink your approach.

Customer feedback also plays a crucial role in iterating and improving. If a particular type of merch isn't resonating, don't double down—pivot. If people rave about a specific item, consider expanding on that idea in future promotions. The best promotional merchandise evolves based on real-world feedback, not just internal assumptions.

Scaling and Evolving for Long-Term Success

Keeping Up with Trends

What worked last year might be irrelevant today. Consumer preferences shift, design trends evolve, and what people once valued can quickly become outdated. Staying ahead means keeping your promotional merchandise fresh, relevant, and desirable.

You don't need to chase every trend, but you do need to recognise the ones that align with your brand and audience. Look at how big brands stay relevant. They don't just follow trends; they set them. Your job is to spot the right movements early and adapt them in a way that feels natural to your identity.

Start by keeping an eye on what's happening in the market. Follow industry publications, watch what your competitors are doing (and more importantly, what your customers are responding to), and use social listening tools to track shifts in consumer behaviour. If sustainable products are gaining traction, consider integrating them into your merchandise. If minimalistic design is dominating, rethink how your branding appears on products.

Data is your best ally here. Analyse what's selling, what's being used, and what's being forgotten in a drawer. If certain types of merchandise are consistently performing well, find ways to refresh them rather than replacing them entirely. A classic example is branded clothing—if t-shirts have worked for you, maybe it's time to experiment with embroidered sweatshirts or performance wear.

The key is to evolve without alienating your existing audience. Change too drastically, and you risk losing brand consistency. Stay too static, and you'll fade into irrelevance. The balance lies in maintaining your core identity while making strategic updates that meet modern demands.

Testing New Merch Concepts

Before going all in on a new idea, validate it. The worst thing you can do is invest in thousands of units of a product that nobody wants. Testing eliminates guesswork and ensures that your promotional merchandise actually resonates with your audience.

Start small. Instead of ordering a massive batch, do a limited run and gauge the response. Sell it, give it away selectively, or distribute it to a test group. Track engagement—are people excited? Are they using it? Is it being shared on social media? If the response is lukewarm, tweak the design or try a different approach before committing to a full production run.

One effective way to test new concepts is through exclusive drops. Offer a limited number of items to your most engaged customers and see how they respond. If they go quickly and people are asking for more, you've got a winner. If they sit untouched, it might be time to rethink your approach.

Feedback loops are crucial here. Ask your customers directly—what do they think? Would they prefer a different colour, size, or functionality? Use surveys, social media polls, and direct conversations to gather insights. The more data you have, the better your decisions will be.

Also, don't be afraid to experiment with unconventional ideas. Some of the most successful promotional merchandise campaigns have come from thinking outside the box. The companies that win aren't just the ones that do what's expected; they're the ones that create something different—something people actually want to talk about.

Expanding Beyond Giveaways into Product Lines

If your promotional merchandise is resonating, why stop at giveaways? Turning your merch into an actual product line can open up an entirely new revenue stream while deepening your brand's connection with your audience.

Look at brands that have successfully done this. Gymshark started with branded fitness clothing and built an empire. Red Bull turned their promotional branding into an entire lifestyle. Even luxury fashion houses release limited-edition merchandise to create buzz and exclusivity.

The first step is identifying which products have strong demand. If people are willing to pay for something you originally gave away, that's a clear signal. Limited edition items, high-quality clothing, and unique accessories are often good starting points.

Once you identify a potential product, treat it like any other business venture—market it properly. Create anticipation. Build a wait list. Use influencers or brand advocates to generate demand. The more exclusivity and desirability you build around it, the more successful it will be.

Selling merchandise doesn't mean you abandon promotional giveaways altogether. Instead, you create a tiered system where some products remain exclusive gifts, while others are available for purchase. The key is giving people a reason to engage at different levels—whether it's as a loyal fan who gets freebies, or as a paying customer who wants more.

This transition from promotional merchandise to a full-fledged product line isn't just about making money; it's about creating deeper engagement. When customers actively seek out and purchase your merchandise, they're not just promoting your brand—they're investing in it.

UNLOCKING THE FULL POTENTIAL OF STRATEGIC MERCHANDISE

"The secret of success is to do the common thing uncommonly well."
– John D. Rockefeller

You've made it this far, which means you're serious about using promotional merchandise as more than just a gimmick. You're not here to waste money on throwaway swag that ends up in the trash. You're here to create a system—one that builds brand recognition, deepens customer loyalty, and fuels revenue growth.

The difference between brands that thrive with merchandise and those that fail isn't luck. It's strategy. You've seen how the right products, in the right hands, at the right time can generate powerful results. Now, it's time to put it all into action.

WHY THIS MATTERS MORE THAN EVER

The marketplace is louder than ever. Consumers are hit with thousands of ads every day. Digital marketing is over saturated. Social media algorithms change on a whim. Email open rates are declining. Attention spans are shrinking.

But a tangible, well-crafted product in someone's hands? That cuts through the noise.

Physical merchandise creates an emotional and sensory experience that digital marketing never can. People don't form a connection with an email or a banner ad. They form connections with things they can touch, use, and integrate into their daily lives.

The brands that understand this aren't just handing out freebies—they're embedding themselves into the routines, habits, and emotions of their audience.

THE DIFFERENCE BETWEEN THROWAWAY SWAG AND BRAND ASSETS

There are two types of promotional merchandise: disposable junk and powerful brand assets.

The first kind is what most businesses do—cheap pens, low-quality t-shirts, random trinkets that nobody remembers. These items don't build relationships. They don't drive sales. They don't create impact.

The second kind is what successful brands do—carefully curated, high-quality merchandise that people actually want. Products that align with the brand's identity. Items that customers use, talk about, and share. These aren't just promotional products; they're extensions of the brand experience.

Every product you put into the world is a representation of

your brand. If it's forgettable, so is your business. If it's valuable, your brand becomes more valuable in the eyes of your customers.

THE REAL RETURN ON INVESTMENT

Promotional merchandise isn't just a cost—it's an asset that generates returns in multiple ways:

- **Brand Awareness That Lasts** – Unlike digital ads that disappear in seconds, physical merchandise stays in people's lives. A well-designed hoodie, a premium water bottle, or a sleek notebook can be seen hundreds of times by a single person—and even more by those around them.
- **Deeper Customer Relationships** – Reciprocity is a powerful psychological trigger. When you give someone something useful and valuable, they feel an unconscious pull toward your brand. This builds goodwill and keeps your business top of mind.
- **Higher Sales and Conversions** – Whether it's through lead generation, loyalty rewards, or influencer collaborations, branded merchandise can be the missing link in turning potential customers into paying ones.
- **A Competitive Edge** – Most businesses treat promotional merchandise as an afterthought. When you do it right, you stand out. You become the brand that people remember, talk about, and choose over the competition.

TAKING ACTION: TURNING STRATEGY INTO RESULTS

Now it's on you. You have the blueprint. You understand the principles. The only thing left is execution.

Start by defining your objectives. What do you want your merchandise to achieve? Awareness? Customer retention? Sales? Then, align your product selection with your audience. What do they actually want? What will they appreciate and use?

Invest in quality over quantity. A single well-made item can have more impact than a hundred cheap giveaways. Prioritize design. Make it aesthetically pleasing, functional, and aligned with your brand's personality.

Be intentional with distribution. Don't just give things away— create experiences around your merchandise. Use scarcity and exclusivity to build demand. Make every item feel like a reward, not an obligation.

And most importantly, track your results. Test different approaches, measure engagement, and refine your strategy over time. The brands that succeed are the ones that adapt, evolve, and continuously improve.

NEED HELP? LET'S MAKE IT HAPPEN TOGETHER

If you're ready to take promotional merchandise seriously but want expert guidance, you don't have to do it alone. Whether you need help choosing the right products, designing merch that resonates, or crafting a full-scale distribution strategy, we're here to help.

Reach out at **www.probospromotions.com** and let's build a merchandise strategy that doesn't just "give stuff away" but actually grows your brand, engages your customers, and drives real results.

The opportunity is in front of you. Now it's time to take action.

Printed in Great Britain
by Amazon